CELESTIAL SEASONINGS®
— COOKBOOK —

Cooking with Tea

by Jennifer and Mo Siegel
with Jordan Simon

PARK
LANE
PRESS

New York • New Jersey

This 1996 edition is published by Park Lane Press, a division of Random House Value Publishing, Inc., 40 Engelhard Avenue, Avenel, New Jersey 07001.

Park Lane Press and colophon are registered trademarks of Random House Value Publishing, Inc.

Random House
New York • Toronto • London • Sydney • Auckland
Printed and bound in Singapore

BOOK DESIGN BY RENATO STANISIC
PHOTOGRAPHS BY MICHAEL LICHTER, BOULDER, CO
FOOD STYLING BY JAQUELINE BUCKNER
TABLEWARE PROVIDED BY THE PEPPERCORN STORE, BOULDER, CO
ADDITIONAL TABLEWARE/PROPS SUPPLIED BY ED PARENT AND ASSOC.
ADDITIONAL PHOTOS BY CHRIS MEAD AND JOSHUA GREENE

Library of Congress Cataloging-in-Publication Data
Siegel, Jennifer.
        Celestial Seasonings cooking with tea / by Jennifer and Mo Siegel.
                p. cm.
        ISBN 0-517-20014-7
        1. Cookery (Tea) I. Siegel, Mo. II. Celestial Seasonings (Firm) III. Title.
TX817.T3S54 1996
641.6'372—dc20   95-47794
                                        CIP

8 7 6 5 4 3 2 1

Acknowledgments

Cooking With Tea has been such a fun project and has made this a wonderful and flavorful year.

The most difficult part of creating this book has been to fit all of the acknowledgments on to one page but here goes!

I'd like to thank all of the great cooks in my life who taught me to take risks such as discovering that tahini in guacamole is great and mayonnaise in mashed potatoes is a must. Therefore, the transition to cooking with tea was a natural one. Thank you to all of my friends and neighbors who were always available to taste and critique. Thank you John and Leslie Lovett for your home, your stuff, your taste-buds and your friendship. Thank you Lindsay Moore and Suzanne Sarto for your artistic Celestial eyes. Thank you Ramona Cappello for your marketing vision for this project. Thank you Patty Bardenett for your desserts. Thank you Sherry Dickerson for your help and kindness. Thank you Doris Hoagland and Eva Shillo at the Peppercorn for all the tableware. Your generosity was overwhelming and without the Peppercorn this book wouldn't be beautiful and Boulder, Colorado wouldn't be complete. Thank you Michael Lichter for the exquisite food photography and thank you Jaqueline Buckner for making even the simplest dish a work of art. Thank you Ed Parent for loaning us some of your treasures.

Thank you Chris Mead for allowing us to see things the way you do—"herbally." Thank you Renato Stanisic for your creative design work. Thank you Bill Huelster, John Groton and everyone at Random House for your belief in this project. Thank you Jordan Simon for your love of food, sense of humor and way with words. Thank you Kate Hartson for everything! You are a talented woman and a good friend.

Thank you Mother for always telling me "there's nothing you can't do," and Dad for believing it. Thank you Kate and Lucas for your love and patience while Mommy cooked.

And...Thank you Mo for being the love of my life.

Contents

Celestial Recipes
15

Hors d'Oeuvres
Soups, Salads &
Side Dishes
Main Courses
Desserts

Iced Teas,
Hot Teas & Happy Teas
112

Celestial
Seasonings Teas
127

Why Cook with Tea? Jen's Story

I'm not a formally trained chef. But my mother did set a good example. She cooked a hearty four-course meal, from salad to dessert, every night of our lives without making a big fuss. When I married Mo, I became an instant mother and short-order cook to his three children—Gabe, Sarah, and Megan. I quickly learned that the best way to my step-kids' hearts was through their stomachs. Soon afterward, I had my own children, Kate and Lucas. Suddenly, I didn't have time to prepare extravagant dinners. I was too busy changing diapers and preventing Lucas from sticking forks in electrical outlets (his favorite hobby). My new rule was if it took more than half an hour to make, forget it. And if it wasn't in the pantry, it didn't go on the table.

But being a parent doesn't mean you stop wanting fine food. And just because my time is limited, doesn't mean my family's taste buds are. One day while standing in my kitchen steaming carrots for the five-millionth time, I decided to throw a couple of Mandarin Orange Spice tea bags in the boiling water. I was surprised at how much the orange and clove in the tea enhanced the flavor of plain old

carrots. A few days later while baking yet another chicken, I stuffed it with several Almond Sunset tea bags. The flavor of the tea steamed the chicken from the inside out. I was onto something.

Most of us have five or six spices we use all the time. Over the years, that can get pretty boring. Celestial Seasonings teas became the spice rack I didn't know I had. Let's face it, who has time to travel to a Moroccan spice market or traipse through the Rockies to pick chamomile flow-

ers at their peak? Celestial Seasonings does it for me.

When I started cooking with tea, I found I was able to create rich ethnic food flavors in my own home that I thought I could only get in restaurants. The herbs and spices in the Celestial Seasonings blends will also enable you to expand your repertoire of international dishes. Even classics that we all grew up with can be reinvented with tea, such as good old-fashioned Yankee pot roast reborn as Cranberry Cove Beef Roast.

Many gourmet recipes have a list of ingredients so long that you spend half a day shopping, half a day cooking, and half a paycheck buying them. By adding tea bags to a simple recipe, you can cook with as many as fourteen exotic herbs and spices you would never have used otherwise. It's cost-and time-efficient: 20 cents and 20 minutes buys you gourmet results. For example, here's what you'd be adding to our simple Mandarin Orange Spice Carrots recipe (page 56) if you didn't use a Mandarin Orange Spice tea bag:

orange peel, hibiscus flowers, roasted chicory root, rosehips, blackberry leaves, chamomile flowers, hawthorn berries, cinnamon, cloves and coriander. Unrealistic expectations for any home chef!

People are always asking me, "Jen, can you really taste the tea in your dishes?" Let me say that for this cookbook, if the tea didn't truly enrich the flavor, the recipe didn't make the book. When cooking with tea, please feel free to experiment. For example, if you really love the flavors in a particular tea, you may consider adding an extra teabag to the recipe. For a lighter flavor, use one less teabag.

But please remember to always be careful when removing a tea bag from hot liquid. I have found that the best way is to use two tablespoons, squeezing out the excess tea between them.

Celestial Seasonings: Mo's Story

Since you are reading this book, you probably love tea, good food, and plants. Me, too! I've loved plants for as long as I can remember. I grew up in Palmer Lake, Colorado, population 500, a tiny mountain town tucked away in the glorious Rockies. As a kid, I picked wild berries in the mountains and sold them for homemade jelly. As an adult, I loved tea, tea, and more tea — and gardens, pine trees laden with fresh mountain snowfalls, and anything related to new and wonderful uses for nature's botanicals.

Since childhood, another love of my life has been art. When I was eighteen, I opened a small art store, selling the Pop Art posters so popular in the '60s and '70s. Being a total health food fanatic, the business evolved into a gallery/health food store. When customers walked in, we served them a free cup of Oriental herb tea. While this was the best blend on the market, it didn't take long to realize that you could have better tea if it were created from the wild herbs in the surrounding mountains.

As I hiked through the Rocky Mountains outside of

*The early days of
Celestial Seasonings
—at the plant and
Mo gathering herbs
in the meadow.*

Aspen that summer, I discovered many different herbs growing wild in the highlands. In three months, I learned to identify, harvest, cure, and blend those plants into comforting tea. The next year, in Boulder, Colorado, some friends and I combed the mountains in search of more herbs. We gathered wild spearmint, chamomile flowers, red clover blossoms, raspberry leaves, rose hips, nettles— 36 different ingredients in all. We harvested 19 bales of herb tea that summer. Being penniless, we couldn't afford drying equipment. Instead, we cleaned old screen doors,

placed logs beneath them, and nailed wood boards to their sides. These contraptions served as drying racks, allowing sun and wind to cure the herbs naturally. It was hardly scientific but it worked. Then I sold the whole batch to a health food store to finance a trip to South America.

Upon my return, I was totally surprised that the store had named the tea MO'S 36 HERB TEA and was distributing it throughout Colorado. It was a hit! I was 20 years old and wondering what to do with my life. Then I met my lifetime friend, John Hay. We teamed up to go into the tea business full-time. John had an MBA, $500 in equity from selling his sports car, and a gift for starting new companies. But what to name our new company? Lucinda Ziesing, our first investor, was nicknamed "Celestial Seasonings" in high school (the guys thought she was from heaven). From the first time I heard that magical name, our company was born.

The first 1,700 Celestial Seasonings cloth bags were cut from muslin with pinking shears and sewn together on an old Singer sewing machine. Then, Mountain Bell donated their scrap telephone cables. The copper filaments inside were insulated in bright, multi-colored plastic, perfect for twist-tying the first 10,000 packages. From the beginning, the packages had art and writing on them, just like our boxes today. The idea for Celestial was always more than tea. It was meant to be delicious tea wrapped in art and loaded with inspirational and sometimes goofy sayings.

We hand-stamped those first muslin tea bags with the price-marker ink used on beef. I figured if people could actually eat it, it was safe enough to stamp on the outside of our bags. I'll never forget my first sales call. I hopped into my little smashed-up Datsun with a tea rack on the roof painted in psychedelic "flower power" colors. Then I drove east with samples of (the newly concocted) Mo's 24 Herb Tea and Red Zinger. I walked into the nearest health food store in Chicago and my pitch was, "We're gonna be the biggest herb tea company in the U.S. in three years, and this is our first product." The store owner was holding one of our bags in his sweaty hand as I gave him the spiel while sticking a container of aromatic Red Zinger under his nose. What I didn't know then was that the ink was water soluble. The store owner held up his hand and, lo and behold, you could read all 24 ingredients on his palm! Back to the drawing board.

Beth Hay, a wonderful artist, was a vital catalyst in our early years. Beth had an artistic vision for the look and feel of Celestial packaging. Our official symbol to this day, the Sleepytime Bear, was created and painted by Beth. From the beginning, Celestial Seasonings has been a collaboration of artists, botanists, tea merchants, and business people. And even though we haven't used screen doors and muslin bags for many years, we still make your teas with the same love and fervor.

Celestial Seasonings is all about plants. We love you to drink them in your tea, eat them in your food, and take herbal extracts when you're sick. And I'm not talking about tomatoes—I'm talking about the stuff with the fancy Latin names. We are the leaves in your trees, the flowers in your garden, the weeds by the side of your road, and the roots underneath your feet.

Celestial Seasonings remains in pursuit of the perfect tea. Tea is beautiful business, like fine wine. When you see

Celestial Seasonings Tea Company, Boulder, Colorado

hibiscus on the label, it's not just hibiscus, it's the best hibiscus! Hibiscus, or any plant, is a variable crop that, according to soil, climate, harvesting time, and country of origin, will have different properties. Celestial's blessed with remarkably sensitive tasters who can spot a tasty flower a mile off. These folks devote their career to developing unique and delicious formulas, often with ingredients one wouldn't think taste great—but they do! Celestial blends over 100 herbs, teas, fruits and spices from over 40 countries on five continents, from Argentina to Zaire. You're warmly invited to visit us in Boulder. When you visit, you can be part of the experimental tea-tasting labs. In 1995 alone, over 65,000 people came by to taste tea and tour. Some brands, like Cinnamon Apple Spice, go through hundreds of different formulas before they're perfected. And 99.5% of the flavors we invent never make it to your teacup! Only the best makes the final cut.

I love tea and any beverage that mixes deliciously with tea. For years, I've been blending teas with everything from Bailey's Irish Cream to soda. So the idea of making wacky, wonderful tea drinks—festive ice tea coolers, hot toddies, bedtime relaxers—is nothing new. In fact I was thrilled to create new drinks for this book. But Raspberry Zinger salad dressing? Strawberry Kiwi tuna? Chamomile cauliflower soup? The first time Jen cooked with tea, I was very skeptical. Sure, it sounded interesting and made sense; after all, we work so hard to create

sophisticated flavors. But as seasonings in food? Yes! I was amazed at how fantastic and healthy Jen's recipes were! And so was our family. With five children, Jen's test recipes were constantly scrutinized. You know how finicky kids' taste buds can be. Yet every one of them—from my oldest, Gabe who's 24, to our five-year-old son, Lucas—loves Jen's tea-based dishes.

Cooking with tea takes Celestial Seasonings teas to a new level. Our mission has always been to help you live a healthier lifestyle while experiencing great taste. Now tea can improve your day through what you drink and by what you eat, too. Thanks, Jen.

Hors d'Oeuvres

Who doesn't love hors d'oeuvres? My mother served them at every important dinner party and neighborhood gathering. Is there anything more welcoming to family and friends than a beautiful platter of goodies? In a little more time than it takes to unwrap a wedge of cheese and some crackers, you can serve your guests a dish that was made with love.

Mandarin Orange Spice Meatballs

SERVES 10

Traditional sweet-and-sour meatballs are always a hit. The clove in the tea makes this recipe delightfully different.

5 Mandarin Orange Spice tea bags

1 ½ cups white wine

1 pound ground beef

1 pound ground pork

¼ red onion, diced

1 tablespoon crushed garlic (4 cloves)

2 tablespoons olive or corn oil

1 tablespoon corn starch

1 cup orange marmalade

Pinch of salt

Dash of pepper

Steep the tea bags in the wine for 10 minutes. Discard the bags and set the wine aside. Blend the beef, pork, onion, garlic, salt, and pepper in a large bowl. Pour 3/4 cup of the wine into the meat and mix well. Form into small meatballs (yields 35-40 meatballs). Heat the oil in a large skillet over medium flame, and brown the meatballs. Remove the meatballs and set aside on a warm platter. Carefully pour the grease out of the skillet. Add the remaining wine, the cornstarch and the marmalade to the skillet. Stir over medium heat until thickened. Add the meatballs and simmer 15 minutes.

PREPARATION TIME: 20 MINUTES

COOKING TIME: 30 MINUTES

Harvest Spice Meatballs

SERVES 6

> "Bread and water can so easily be toast and tea."
>
> —Maela Moore

Here is a perfect example of how using tea can really enhance your cooking. Harvest Spice is one of our most pungent, aromatic teas. The peppery cinnamon flavor will convince your guests that you've mastered Mediterranean cooking. The meatballs can also be served as an entree.

2 Harvest Spice tea bags

2 tablespoons white vinegar

3 tablespoons water

1 pound ground pork

1 tablespoon diced garlic
    (4 cloves)

1 teaspoon dried oregano

1 teaspoon chili powder

½ teaspoon salt

½ cup crumbled feta cheese

2 tablespoons olive oil

Steep the tea bags in the vinegar and cold water for 10 minutes. Combine the remaining ingredients except the oil in a large bowl. Remove the tea bags, squeezing excess liquid into bowl; then discard the bags. Add the tea mixture to the meat mixture and blend thoroughly. Form 12 to 15 meatballs. Heat the oil in a large skillet over medium heat. Sauté for 10 to 15 minutes, or until cooked through. Serve with Harvest Spice Meatball Dipping Sauce (see following recipe).

PREPARATION TIME:
20 MINUTES
COOKING TIME:
10 TO 15 MINUTES

Harvest Spice Meatball Dipping Sauce

SERVES 3 (6 APPETIZER PORTIONS)

1 Harvest Spice tea bag

2 tablespoons white vinegar

1 ½ cups sour cream

2 tablespoons water

½ teaspoon dried oregano

½ teaspoon coarsely ground black pepper

"Great things are made of little things."

—Robert Browning

Steep the tea bag in cold vinegar for 10 minutes. Gently squeeze out the vinegar, and discard the tea bag. Add the remaining ingredients and mix thoroughly. Serve on the side as a dipping sauce for Harvest Spice Meatball hors d'oeuvres (see preceding recipe) or pour the sauce over the meatballs served as an entrée.

PREPARATION TIME:
15 MINUTES

Brie with Strawberry Kiwi Cranberry Sauce

SERVES 4

When some unexpected guests popped in, I ransacked my fridge for something to serve and found this sauce leftover from a traditional turkey dinner. I love the combination of fruit and cheese, so I heated the sauce and poured it over a wedge of Brie. I've been serving it that way ever since. The tea is just sweet enough to undercut the tartness of the cranberries, and the sauce keeps in your refrigerator for a couple of weeks!

1 cup water	1 cup sugar
3 Strawberry Kiwi tea bags	3 cups whole cranberries
1 pound wheel of brie	½ cup chopped walnuts, optional

Boil the water in a heavy saucepan, and add the tea bags. Simmer, allowing the tea to steep for 5 minutes. Then remove and discard the bags. Add the remaining sugar and cranberries and simmer for 1 hour, stirring every 10 minutes. Pour over the brie and garnish, if desired, with walnuts. Let the cheese stand at room temperature for 1/2 hour before serving.

"Earth's crammed with Heaven."
—Elizabeth Barrett Browning

PREPARATION TIME: 10 MINUTES

COOKING TIME: 1 HOUR

Apricot Ginger Wonton Dipping Sauce

SERVES 4 TO 6

3 tablespoons water

½ cup light soy sauce

1 Apricot Ginger tea bag

"Life begets life. Energy creates energy. It is by spending oneself that one becomes rich."

—Sarah Bernhardt

Combine the water, soy sauce, and tea bag, and let steep for 20 minutes. Remove the tea bag, squeezing excess liquid into the sauce; then discard the bag. Serve as a dipping sauce for Peppermint Thai Dumplings (recipe follows).

PREPARATION TIME:
20 MINUTES

Peppermint Thai Dumplings

SERVES 4 TO 6

Trust me, this is much easier than it sounds. These days you can buy wonton skins in the produce department of your supermarket. You can also buy wonton makers in Asian grocers—they make perfect wontons with no effort.

4 ½ cups water

6 Peppermint tea bags

1 pound ground pork or turkey

2 tablespoons diced scallions

2 tablespoons wok oil

20 wonton skins

¼ cup Apricot Ginger Wonton Dipping Sauce
   (see preceeding recipe)

Bring 1/2 cup of water to a boil and add 2 of the tea bags. Steep for 5 minutes and remove the tea bags, squeezing excess liquid into the tea; then discard the bags. Combine the tea, ground pork or turkey, scallions, and wok oil, and blend well. Place 2 tablespoons of the mixture on each wonton skin and fold up the sides. Place the remaining 4 tea bags in the 4 cups water, and bring to a boil in the bottom part of a steamer. Place the wontons on the top half of the steamer and steam for 15 to 20 minutes, or until cooked through.

"Light tomorrow with today."

—Elizabeth Barrett Browning

PREPARATION TIME:
30 MINUTES

COOKING TIME:
20 MINUTES

Harvest Spice Veggie Dip

SERVES 4 to 6

"One changes from day to day ... every few years one becomes a new being."

—George Sand

Just say no to fat and salt! Throw away your sour cream-and-onion dip! This rendition is so good they should flavor a potato chip after it.

2 Harvest Spice tea bags

¼ cup cider vinegar

1 ¼ cups plain low-fat yogurt

2 tablespoons sugar

Steep the tea bags in the vinegar for 10 minutes. Remove and discard the bags. Combine the tea vinegar, yogurt, and sugar in a mixing bowl; stir until blended. Chill for 20 minutes, and serve with carrots, celery, broccoli, cauliflower, and other raw veggies.

PREPARATION TIME:
15 MINUTES

CHILL TIME:
20 MINUTES

Strawberry Kiwi Fruit Dip

I served this as a snack to my daughter Kate's kindergarten class and as an hors d'oeuvre at a grown-ups' luncheon. The kids called it "cool," and the adults pronounced it "fabulous."

2 Strawberry Kiwi tea bags	**15 ounces ricotta cheese**
¾ cup water	**3 tablespoons sugar**

Add the tea bags to the water, bring to a boil, and steep for 10 minutes. Remove and discard the tea bags. Combine the tea, ricotta, and sugar in a bowl, and mix well. Chill for 30 minutes, and serve with the fresh fruit of your choice.

"A man's reach should exceed his grasp, or what's a heaven for?"

—Robert Browning

PREPARATION TIME:
15 MINUTES
CHILL TIME:
30 MINUTES

Mandarin Orange Spice Chicken

SERVES 4

These chicken pieces make nice hors d'oeuvres at a cocktail party, or you can bring them along on a family picnic. You can always tell the kids these are chicken nuggets.

4 Mandarin Orange Spice
   tea bags

4 boneless, skinless chicken
   breasts, cubed into 1-inch
   squares

2 ½ cups water

2 teaspoons crushed garlic
   (3 cloves)

2 tablespoons light soy sauce

½ cup flour

4 tablespoons peanut oil

Combine the tea bags, chicken, water, garlic, and soy sauce. Marinate for at least 3 hours (overnight is best). Remove the chicken, and coat each piece in flour. Sauté the chicken cubes over medium heat in peanut oil until golden brown and cooked through (about 10 minutes).

PREPARATION TIME:
5 MINUTES

MARINATE TIME:
3 HOURS TO
OVERNIGHT

COOKING TIME:
10 MINUTES

Mandarin Orange Spice Dipping Sauce

SERVES 4

½ cup water

2 Mandarin Orange Spice
tea bags

¾ cup orange marmalade

2 teaspoons cornstarch

Boil the water, and steep the tea bags for 5 minutes before removing them. Add the marmalade and cornstarch, reduce heat to medium, and stir continuously until the sauce is thickened (5 to 10 minutes).

"The earth and every common sight to me did seem appareled in celestial light."

—William Wordsworth

COOKING TIME:
15 TO 20 MINUTES

Cranberry Cove Cocktail Meatballs

SERVES 8-10

When I was growing up, we lived down the street from a magical woman named Khairul. At a time when everyone made the same safe, boring dishes, Khairul loved to experiment. She was the first person on the block to make paella and other exotic dishes. So I was delighted when she agreed to create a recipe for this book. As soon as the meatballs started sizzling in my frying pan, the aroma conjured memories of Khairul's New Year's Eve parties, when we never knew what wonders would emerge from her kitchen.

PREPARATION TIME:
30 MINUTES

COOKING TIME:
35 MINUTES

3 Cranberry Cove tea bags

1 cup water

1 12 oz. can cranberry sauce

½ cup ketchup

1 teaspoon brown sugar

¾ teaspoon black pepper

1 pound chopped beef (round
   steak is best)

1 small onion, chopped

1 clove garlic, chopped

1 egg

1 teaspoon salt

1 tablespoon Worcestershire sauce

½ cup dried bread crumbs

Steep the tea bags in cold water for 5 minutes. Remove and discard the bags. Combine the tea, cranberry sauce, ketchup, brown sugar, and 1/4 teaspoon of the pepper in a medium-sized saucepan. Heat over medium heat, stirring until the sugar is melted and the ingredients are blended.

Combine the rest of the ingredients in a large bowl, and mix well. Form into meatballs the size of walnuts (approximately 40). Place the meatballs in a shallow glass baking dish, large enough to accommodate them in one layer. Pour the sauce over the meatballs, making sure they are all covered. Bake at 375 degrees for 35 minutes, turning the meatballs over after the first 20 minutes.

Last year for Mother's Day, my daughter surprised me with a lovely assortment of tea sachets. She found some bits of unused lace in my sewing kit, put a different tea bag in each, and tied them up with her hair ribbons. Pretty cute, huh?

Soups

Warm and comforting in winter, brisk and refreshing in summer, soups are a wonderful start to any meal, or can be a meal in themselves. With tea as a main seasoning ingredient, these soups taste complex but are really very simple to prepare. For even more flavor, use less salt and more tea!

Bengal Spice Mushroom Soup

SERVES 4

Today almost every produce market carries a wide assortment of mushrooms: portobellos, shiitakes, enokis. . . . whatever you want, you can find. The Bengal Spice tea makes this soup taste like you've added a thousand and one herbs and spices from around the world. It's so simple yet so elegant.

1 diced shallot

2 large portobello mushrooms, cubed

2 cups sliced button mushrooms

2 tablespoons butter

4 cups water

4 Bengal Spice tea bags

1 cup heavy cream

2 tablespoons cornstarch

Salt and pepper

Sauté the shallot and mushrooms in butter until tender. Bring the water to a boil in a saucepan, and add the tea bags. Lower to a simmer, and steep the tea bags for 5 minutes. Remove and discard the tea bags. Add the cream to the tea; then whisk in cornstarch. Return to a boil over medium heat until thickened. Then add the mushrooms and shallots and salt and pepper to taste.

"Everything beautiful impresses us as sufficient to itself."

—Henry David Thoreau

PREPARATION TIME: 10 MINUTES

COOKING TIME: 15 MINUTES

Chamomile Chicken Soup

What is more comforting to serve someone who isn't feeling well than chicken soup or chamomile tea? So why not both?

1 whole skinless chicken	4 cups chopped celery (7 to 8 stalks)
7 ½ quarts water	2 large yellow onions, chopped
12 Chamomile tea bags	4 cups chopped carrots (7 to 8 carrots)
4 cups chopped cauliflower (approximately 2 small heads)	1 cup rice (white or brown)

Place the chicken and water in a large stockpot. Boil until cooked through (about 50 minutes). Remove the chicken and set aside to cool. When cool, remove the chicken meat from the bone. Cut into bite-sized pieces. Add the tea bags to the broth, bring to a boil for 7 minutes, and then remove and discard the bags. Add the chicken, cauliflower, celery, onions, carrots, and rice to the pot. Add salt and pepper to taste. Simmer on low heat for approximately 2 hours.

For a delightful bath, instead of throwing in expensive artificial bath beads, try adding a couple of chamomile tea bags to the water. It's aromatherapy made easy!

PREPARATION TIME: 30 MINUTES

COOKING TIME: 2 HOURS

Bengal Spice Shrimp Bisque

SERVES 4

> "All that is gold does not glitter. All who wander are not lost."
>
> —J.R.R. Tolkien

Is there any more elegant soup than a bisque? This makes a dynamite start to an important dinner party. But the Bengal Spice flavors are so complex and the texture so satiny smooth that you can even serve it as the entrée at a luncheon with a side of green salad.

8 Bengal Spice tea bags

3 cups cold water

1 pound medium raw shrimp, peeled and deveined

¾ cup diced yellow onions (1 small–medium onion)

1 cup chopped green peppers (1 large green pepper)

½ cup sliced water chestnuts

1 tablespoon butter

1 pint heavy cream

1 (14 ½ ounce) can chicken broth

½ cup chopped fresh cilantro, for garnish

MARINATE TIME:
2 TO 3 HOURS

PREPARATION TIME:
15 MINUTES

COOKING TIME:
15 MINUTES

Combine the tea bags, water, and shrimp in a large bowl. Cover and refrigerate for 2 to 3 hours. Sauté the onions, peppers, and water chestnuts in butter over medium heat for 5 minutes. Remove the shrimp from the tea marinade and add to the vegetables. Stir in the cream and chicken broth. Cook over low heat until the shrimp is pink and cooked through. Serve in warm bowls and garnish with cilantro. For a more pronounced Indian flavor, add 2 extra tea bags to the cream and chicken broth. Simmer for 5 minutes. Remove and discard the tea bags.

Save your favorite Celestial Seasonings tea box quotes for your next dinner party. Place one underneath each napkin before your guests arrive. It's an inspirational start to a magical night.

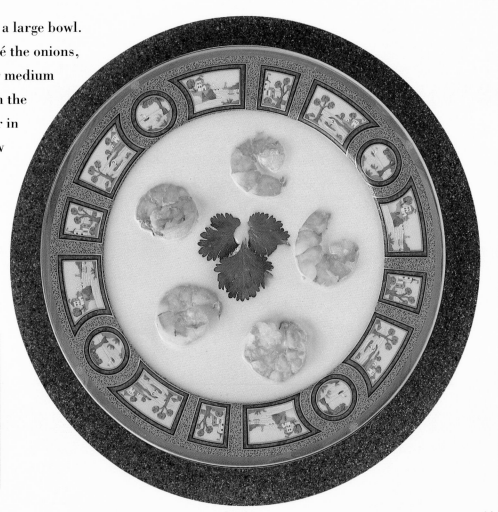

Chamomile Cauliflower Soup

SERVES 4

A dear friend and member of the Celestial board of directors came to our house one evening. After hearing about the book, he suggested, "Why not try steaming cauliflower in chamomile? If nothing else, the words will look good together in print." We all laughed. Little did I know that this would turn out to be one of my favorite recipes in the entire book: low in fat, high in flavor. Thanks, Ron!

6 Chamomile tea bags

3 cups water

1 large head of cauliflower,
   cut into three pieces

¼ cup chopped onions

2 celery stalks, chopped

2 tablespoons butter

Salt and pepper

Place the tea bags and water in a soup pot and bring to a boil. Let the tea bags steep for 5 minutes and then discard them. Add the cauliflower, cover, and cook for 15 minutes, or until tender. In a shallow pan, sauté the onions and celery in butter until the onions are clear. Place the cauliflower with its liquid and the sautéed vegetables in a blender or food processor. Purée until smooth. Add salt and pepper, and serve.

PREPARATION TIME:
15 MINUTES

COOKING TIME:
25 TO 35 MINUTES

Mandarin Orange Spice Carrot Soup

SERVES 4 TO 6

Rich in color, rich in flavor, rich in vitamins, this soup is terrific served either hot or cold. For a more elegant presentation, try floating a thin curl of orange rind on top; or add a dollop of orange yogurt.

PREPARATION TIME:
30 MINUTES

COOKING TIME:
30 TO 40 MINUTES

1 quart water

11 Mandarin Orange Spice
 tea bags

3 pounds carrots, peeled and sliced

3 cups milk, or half-and-half

2 teaspoons sugar

Place the water and 10 of the tea bags in a large pot; bring to a boil. After 5 minutes, remove the tea bags. Add the carrots to the tea, lower the heat to medium, and cover tightly. Cook until the carrots are tender (about 30 minutes). Bring the milk or half-and-half to a boil in a saucepan. Add the sugar and the last tea bag; remove from heat and steep for 5 minutes. Discard the tea bag. Pour the milk into the carrots. Purée the soup in batches in a blender until smooth, and serve.

Green Pea Mint Soup

SERVES 4

Fresh mint is sometimes hard to find. Using this tea gives you all the flavor of a wild mint field, as though you went out picking in the morning before breakfast and simmered the leaves all day long.

3 Peppermint tea bags

2 ½ cups water

4 cups green peas (2 10-ounce packages frozen or 1 pound fresh, shucked)

2 teaspoons sugar

1 cup milk

Salt and pepper

Plain yogurt or creme fraiche, optional

PREPARATION TIME:
30 MINUTES
COOKING TIME:
20 TO 30 MINUTES

Place the tea bags and the water in a heavy saucepan, and bring to a boil. Continue steeping on high heat for 4 minutes. Remove the tea bags. Add the peas and sugar, and simmer for 15 minutes. Purée the mixture in a blender or food processor until smooth. Return the soup to the saucepan. Stir in the milk over medium heat until blended. Add salt and pepper to taste. Serve topped with a dollop of yogurt or creme fraiche.

English Breakfast Onion Soup

SERVES 4

Here's a healthier version of an old favorite. It contains less salt, less beef, and less fat than a traditional French onion soup, but just as much flavor. The English Breakfast is so rich and dense, you don't even need to top this soup with cheese.

3 large yellow onions, thinly sliced

3 tablespoons butter

1 teaspoon flour

2 cups beef broth

2 cups water

4 English Breakfast tea bags

¼ cup red wine

1 teaspoon salt

Sauté the onions in butter over medium heat until very clear (about 20 minutes). Stir in the flour, and lower the heat. Meanwhile, bring the beef broth, wine, and water to a boil in a separate pot. Add the tea bags and salt, and simmer for 5 minutes. Remove the tea bags. Add the liquid to the onions, cover, and cook for 1 hour over low heat.

"A mind that is stretched to a new idea never returns to its original dimension."

—Oliver Wendell Holmes

PREPARATION TIME: 30 MINUTES

COOKING TIME: 1 HOUR

Salads & Dressings

I saw a fancy bottle of mango vinaigrette in a gourmet store in Aspen, Colorado. Not only did the list of ingredients read like a science experiment, with all manner of artificial flavorings, but I just about fainted when I saw the price. You can make something better and far healthier for the cost of four Celestial Seasonings tea bags and one cup of plain white vinegar. I hope you have as much fun creating these salads and dressings as I did!

Lemon Zinger Vinaigrette Tuna Salad

SERVES 4

After trying this dressing over tuna, you'll never use mayonnaise again.

½ cup cider vinegar

2 Lemon Zinger tea bags

1 cup light oil (such as vegetable or canola)

1 teaspoon dried basil

¼ teaspoon sugar

1 head iceberg lettuce, chopped

½ cup sunflower seeds

1 large can (12 ½ oz.) water-packed white tuna

Place the vinegar and tea bags in a jar, and steep for 20 minutes. Remove the tea bags, and squeeze the excess liquid into the jar before discarding the bag. Add the oil, basil, and sugar, and shake well. Combine the remaining ingredients in a large salad bowl; toss with the dressing. Chill for 15 minutes, and serve.

"Creativity demands nothing less than all you have."

—Erica Jong

PREPARATION TIME:
30 MINUTES
CHILL TIME:
15 MINUTES

Orange Mango Zinger Shrimp Salad

Caribbean cooking is something we thought we could only get on vacation. But with this tea, you can bring the Tropics home with you. The deep green of the chives and dill against the bright colors of the pink shrimp and orange mango make this salad a feast for the eyes, as well as the palate.

> "Celestial wisdom calms the mind."
>
> —Samuel Johnson

5 cups water

5 Orange Mango Zinger tea bags

1 ½ pounds shrimp, peeled and deveined

½ cup white vinegar

1 cup olive oil

1 tablespoon Dijon mustard

2 tablespoons dill (fresh is preferable)

1 ½ tablespoons chopped chives

1 large mango, peeled and diced

1 head romaine lettuce, cut into 2-inch pieces

PREPARATION TIME:
40 MINUTES

CHILL TIME:
15 MINUTES

Place the water and 3 of the tea bags in a large pot, and boil for 5 minutes. Remove and discard the tea bags. Add the shrimp and cook until pink. Drain and set the shrimp aside. Place the vinegar and the other 2 tea bags in a jar and steep for 15 minutes. Remove and discard the bags. Add the olive oil, mustard, dill, and chives to the vinegar. Shake well. Combine the shrimp, mango, and dressing. Chill for 15 minutes. Then pour over a bed of romaine.

Raspberry Zinger Vinaigrette

This vinaigrette is the first salad dressing I ever made, and it's still my favorite. It took years for Celestial Seasonings to perfect this raspberry blend, but in twenty minutes you can have the perfect dressing. Try serving this over romaine with some blue cheese crumbled on top.

2 Raspberry Zinger tea bags

½ cup white vinegar

¾ cup olive oil

1 teaspoon balsamic vinegar

1 teaspoon sugar

Place the tea bags and vinegar in a jar. Steep the tea bags for 20 minutes. Remove the bags, and gently squeeze the last bit of flavor from the bags before discarding. Add the remaining ingredients to the vinegar, and shake.

"Familiar acts are beautiful through love."

—Percy Bysshe Shelley

PREPARATION TIME:
20 MINUTES

Lemon Zinger Fruit Salad

SERVES 4

Fruit salad is a healthful, delicious summer dessert. In this variation, the tea adds a lemony zing to the fruit. Your kids will love raiding the fridge for this after-school snack.

4 Lemon Zinger tea bags

1 cup water

3 tablespoons sugar

2 cups ice

4 cups sliced fruit

1 cup vanilla yogurt

Bring the water to a boil and steep the tea bags for 4 minutes. Add the sugar, stir until dissolved, discard the tea bags, and remove from heat. Add the ice and stir until melted. Pour over the fruit and chill for 1 hour. Serve topped with vanilla yogurt.

PREPARATION TIME:
15 MINUTES

CHILL TIME:
1 HOUR

Peppermint Cucumber Salad

SERVES 4

Yogurt, mint, and cucumbers are to Middle Eastern cooking what ranch dressing is to American. To enjoy chilled cucumber soup in the summer, first remove the seeds from the cucumbers. Then prepare the salad. Finally, purée the salad in the blender. Chill and serve in tea cups.

2 Peppermint tea bags

½ cup white vinegar

1 tablespoon sugar

½ cup low-fat or nonfat yogurt

2 large cucumbers, peeled and sliced

Steep the tea bags in the vinegar for 20 minutes. Remove and discard the tea bags. Add the sugar and yogurt. Mix well. Pour the mixture over the sliced cucumbers. Toss and chill for 10 minutes.

"If you tell the truth, you don't have to remember anything."

—Mark Twain

PREPARATION TIME:
30 MINUTES

CHILL TIME:
10 MINUTES

Mint Magic Vinaigrette

PREPARATION TIME:
5 MINUTES

CHILL TIME:
4 HOURS

Who knew mint would make such a terrific salad dressing? Mo did. He suggested I make this, and now it's one of his favorites. For an impressive main course, pour the vinaigrette over thinly sliced lamb laid atop wild greens.

3 Mint Magic tea bags

1 cup olive oil

¾ cup balsamic vinegar

1 garlic clove

½ teaspoon oregano

½ teaspoon black pepper

Pinch of salt

Combine all the ingedients in a jar and refrigerate for at least 4 hours. Remove the tea bags and garlic. Cover and shake well.

Everyone appreciates a homemade gift. I don't have the time (and frankly the talent) to piece a quilt or knit a sweater. So I collect jelly jars and fill them with tea-flavored vinegars. My children and I then cut out labels in the shape of tea cups. They decorate the labels, and I write "Raspberry Zinger Vinegar" or "Orange Mango Vinegar." They make easy, inexpensive, wonderfully sentimental gourmet gifts.

Strawberry Kiwi Spinach Salad

SERVES 4

I love this salad because the colors are just as vivid as the flavor. To serve as a main course, try adding a little goat cheese.

2 Strawberry Kiwi tea bags

½ cup white vinegar

¾ cup olive oil

½ teaspoon sugar

3 cups spinach leaves, stems removed (approximately ½ pound)

¼ cup sliced almonds

½ cup kiwi, peeled and diced (approximately ¼ pound)

½ cup diced strawberries (approximately ¼ pound)

¼ cup crumbled goat cheese, optional

In a jar, steep the tea bags in the vinegar for 20 minutes. Remove and discard the bags. Add the olive oil and sugar, and shake until completely blended. Combine the spinach, almonds, kiwi, and strawberries in a bowl. Pour the dressing over the salad and toss. Add 1/4 cup goat cheese if so desired.

"Character is much easier kept than recovered."

—Thomas Paine

PREPARATION AND
COOKING TIME:
30 MINUTES

Green Tea Oriental Salad And Dressing

SERVES 6

While Mo was seeking the ideal carton design for this new tea, he rummaged through art prints he collected in China fifteen years ago. Suddenly, a beautiful Asian woman stared back at him, but she did look rather sad. Thanks to computers, our art department was able to give her the Mona Lisa smile that graces the tea carton.

3 Emerald Gardens tea bags

½ cup white vinegar

3 tablespoons sesame oil

¼ teaspoon light soy sauce

¼ teaspoon sugar

¾ cup olive oil

4 boneless, skinless chicken breasts

1 head iceberg lettuce chopped

½ cup toasted slivered almonds

1 4-ounce can water chestnuts, strained

PREPARATION AND COOKING TIME: 30 MINUTES

Place the tea bags and vinegar in a jar, and steep for 20 or so minutes. Remove the tea bags and squeeze the excess vinegar into the jar before discarding the tea bags. Add 1 tablespoon of the sesame oil. Add the soy sauce, sugar, and olive oil. Shake well. Meanwhile, heat the remaining 2 tablespoons of sesame oil in a large frying pan. Add the chicken and sauté over medium heat until cooked through (4 to 7 minutes per side). Remove the chicken breasts to a plate, and allow to cool. Tear the chicken into small pieces. In a large salad bowl, combine the lettuce, almonds, chicken, water chestnuts, dressing and toss.

Chicken and Pasta Salad with Creamy Chamomile Dressing

SERVES 4 TO 6

PREPARATION AND
CHILL TIME:
80 MINUTES

Chamomile has a soft, subtle taste that sneaks up on you. Children especially love this salad.

3 Chamomile tea bags

¼ cup white vinegar

¾ cup light mayonnaise

1 ½ teaspoons tarragon, fresh is preferable

1 pound pasta (any variety)

2 tablespoons olive oil

4 boneless, skinless chicken breasts

½ cup diced red peppers (approximately 1 small pepper, or ½ medium)

½ cup diced green peppers (1 small pepper, or ½ medium)

Steep the tea bags in the vinegar for 15 minutes. Squeeze out the excess liquid before discarding the bags. Mix in the mayonnaise and tarragon, and chill. Meanwhile, cook the pasta until al dente (usually 7 to 10 minutes, depending on size). Drain pasta and reserve. Heat the oil in a skillet and sauté the chicken, until it is cooked through (about 10 to 15 minutes). Remove the chicken to a plate to cool. Shred the chicken. Combine the chicken, pasta, peppers, and dressing in a large bowl. Toss and chill.

Bengal Spice Chicken Salad

SERVES 4

PREPARATION AND
CHILL TIME:
1 HOUR

COOKING TIME:
30 TO 40 MINUTES

Remember that old American classic, Waldorf salad, which used to be served at just about every important social luncheon? You can reinvent it with tea. The racy flavors of Bengal Spice set off the grapes, dates, and walnuts beautifully.

4 cups water

4 Bengal Spice tea bags

4 boneless, skinless chicken
   breasts

½ cup chopped walnuts

¾ cup seedless grapes

¼ cup chopped dates

½ cup light mayonnaise

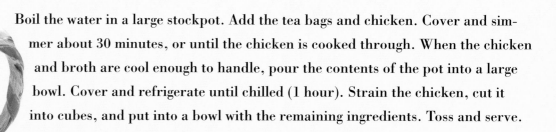

Boil the water in a large stockpot. Add the tea bags and chicken. Cover and simmer about 30 minutes, or until the chicken is cooked through. When the chicken and broth are cool enough to handle, pour the contents of the pot into a large bowl. Cover and refrigerate until chilled (1 hour). Strain the chicken, cut it into cubes, and put into a bowl with the remaining ingredients. Toss and serve.

Side Dishes

Too often, very little attention is paid to preparing the lonely side dish. The star of the show is always the main course, or maybe a fancy dessert. But a meal is only as good as its supporting cast. The addition of tea will make your side dishes really sing.

Mandarin Orange Spice Carrots

SERVES 4

PREPARATION TIME:
10 MINUTES
COOKING TIME:
5 TO 10 MINUTES

This recipe has a lot of sentimental value. It was my first experiment in cooking with tea. Its wonderful orange clove flavor adds a new dimension to plain old carrots. Omit the orange rind and Grand Marnier for a humbler dish.

2 cups water
2 Mandarin Orange Spice tea bags
4 cups carrots, sliced

1 stick (8 tablespoons) unsalted butter
Rind of ½ orange, cut into thin strips
2 tablespoons Grand Marnier liqueur

Boil the water in a medium covered pot. Add the tea bags and steep 4 to 6 minutes. Remove the tea bags and discard. Cook the carrots in the tea until desired tenderness. Drain the carrots and set aside. In the same pot, combine the butter, orange rind, and Grand Marnier, and cook over low heat until the butter melts. Add the carrots, stir, and serve.

Almond Sunset Green Beans

This American classic is even better made with tea. The subtle taste of Almond Sunset enhances the beans, and the almonds add a wonderful crunchy texture.

PREPARATION TIME:
10 MINUTES

COOKING TIME:
4 TO 7 MINUTES

2 cups water

3 Almond Sunset tea bags

1 pound green beans

¼ cup sliced almonds

4 tablespoons butter

Boil the water in a large saucepan and add the tea bags. Let steep for 4 minutes over medium heat. Remove the bags and take the saucepan off the heat. Put the green beans in a steamer. Place the steamer in the saucepan over the tea. Cover and steam over high heat for 4 to 7 minutes (depending on how crunchy you like them). Remove the green beans to a bowl. Add the almonds and butter, toss, and serve.

Chamomile Polenta

PREPARATION AND COOKING TIME: 2 HOURS

Polenta is the perfect comfort food, especially with the chamomile added. This polenta makes a fancy side dish for guests, a delicious treat for your kids and there's nothing more soothing for a toddler. I serve it chilled in summer and warm in winter. Remember to stir continuously, or the polenta will become lumpy (and less appetizing).

6 cups water

3 Chamomile tea bags

1 cup polenta (ground corn meal)

½ stick (4 tablespoons) unsalted butter plus butter for greasing the pan

Salt and pepper

Boil the water in a saucepan. Steep the tea bags in the boiling water for 4 minutes. Remove and discard the bags. Add the polenta and lower the heat to medium. Stir continuously until the polenta has thickened (about 15 minutes). Add the butter and salt and pepper to taste. Pour into a greased baking dish, and refrigerate until firm (at least 1 hour). Serve chilled, or bake at 350 degrees for 25 to 35 minutes, until heated through.

Vanilla Maple Sweet Potatoes

I had been making this dish for years without the tea, and it was always my stepdaughter Megan's favorite. Now with the tea added, the flavors are so rich and decadent that she misses Melrose Place *for dinner!*

10 large sweet potatoes, peeled
   and chopped

1 pint heavy cream

1 stick (8 tablespoons) butter

1 cup maple syrup

8 ounces cream cheese

4 Vanilla Maple tea bags

Boil the sweet potatoes until very tender (about 45 minutes). Drain and set aside in a large bowl. Place the cream, butter, maple syrup, and cream cheese in a heavy saucepan on medium heat. Stir until smooth. Add the tea bags to the cream mixture, and steep for 5 minutes. Remove the bags. Pour the cream mixture over the sweet potatoes and blend.

PREPARATION TIME:
15 MINUTES

COOKING TIME:
1 HOUR

Vanilla Maple Baked Sweet Potatoes

SERVES 1

My godson Paton will eat only spaghetti and sweet potatoes. You can imagine how it drives his mom, Leslie, crazy, preparing old-fashioned sweet potatoes from scratch. I devised this recipe to make her life easier. The vanilla and maple flavors are the ideal marriage for the potato. Now Paton won't eat them any other way and neither will Paton's Dad.

1 sweet potato
1 Vanilla Maple tea bag
Butter

Pinch of sugar
Pinch of cinnamon

Wash the sweet potato thoroughly and slice in half lengthwise. Lay one moistened tea bag between the two halves, and wrap the potato in foil. Pierce with a fork several times (avoiding the tea bag). If the potato is larger, bake at 350 degrees for 1 hour. (Bake for slightly less time if potato is smaller.) Carefully unwrap the hot sweet potato, and remove the tea bag. Butter, sprinkle with sugar and cinnamon, and serve.

PREPARATION TIME:
5 MINUTES

COOKING TIME:
1 HOUR

Almond Sunset Rice

SERVES 4

Simply by throwing a couple of tea bags into your boiling water, you can transform white rice into something special enough for company.

PREPARATION TIME:
10 MINUTES

COOKING TIME:
25 MINUTES

4 cups water

4 Almond Sunset tea bags

2 cups basmati or white rice

¾ stick (6 tablespoons) butter

¼ cup toasted slivered almonds

2 teaspoons sugar

Salt

Bring the water and tea bags to a boil in a saucepan, lower to a simmer, and steep for 5 minutes. Remove and discard the tea bags. Add the rice, cover, and simmer for 20 minutes. Remove the saucepan from the heat. Add the butter, almonds, sugar, and salt to taste. Mix well, cover, and let sit for 5 minutes.

Cranberry Cove Turkey Stuffing

SERVES 4

It's true. America does *love stuffing, and we'd eat it three times a week. But if you knew what went into many of those ordinary, just-add-water stuffings on your supermarket shelf, you'd go back to potatoes. This Cranberry Cove stuffing is just as easy as any instant. But instead of salt and artificial flavors, you're seasoning not only with cranberries but with cinnamon, chamomile, chicory, citrus and that's just the Cs.*

"Trifles make perfection, but perfection is no trifle."

——Michelangelo

PREPARATION TIME:
15 MINUTES

1 ½ cups water

3 Cranberry Cove tea bags

4 cups dried seasoned bread
   stuffing (I use Pepperidge
   Farm)

1 (16-ounce) can whole cranberry sauce

1 teaspoon salt

3 tablespoons unsalted butter

1 medium yellow onion, diced

Boil the water and steep the tea bags for 5 minutes. Remove and discard the bags. Combine the tea, stuffing, cranberry sauce, and salt in a large bowl. Melt the butter in a frying pan. Saute the onions until clear. Add the onions to the stuffing and mix well. Stuff the turkey and bake according to size. *(This amount works for a 7- to 10-pound turkey.)*

Cranberry Cove Turkey Gravy

SERVES 6 TO 8

This gravy is the perfect complement to Cranberry Cove Turkey stuffing. The subtle fruit flavors of cranberries, apples, and dates in this tea will surprise your turkey and your guests.

2 cups turkey drippings

2 Cranberry Cove tea bags

2 tablespoons cornstarch

Salt

½ cup whole cranberries, optional

½ cup chopped walnuts, optional

Pour the drippings into a medium-sized saucepan and add the tea bags. Bring to a boil, lower to a simmer, and steep for 5 minutes. Carefully lift out the tea bags, and gently press the excess liquid into the pot with the back of a spoon. Discard the bags. Combine the cornstarch and water in a jar, shake well, and pour into the drippings. Bring to a boil and cook, stirring occasionally, until thickened. Add salt to taste and, should you desire, cranberries or walnuts or both.

"Our grand business in life is not to see what lies dimly at a distance, but to do what lies clearly at hand."

—Thomas Carlyle

PREPARATION TIME:
10 MINUTES

COOKING TIME:
10 MINUTES

Main Courses

Cooking with tea can shorten your shopping and preparation time, save you money, and add flavor and flair to your meals. Why make a special dinner only on special occasions? Who do we really want to please? The board of directors once a year, or our families every night? The Chinese have cooked poultry with tea for thousands of years, but I've found tea is also delicate enough to pair with any seafood and robust enough to stand up to any beef.

Firelight Orange Spice Duck

SERVES 4 TO 6

Let's face it, duck can be a little intimidating. But what better way to show off your culinary skills?
The wonderfully robust black tea orange flavor saturates the duck and eliminates its gamey taste.

3 cups water

10 Firelight Orange Spice tea bags

4 tablespoons sugar

2 tablespoons cornstarch

¼ cup Grand Marnier liqueur or brandy

1 cup low-sugar orange marmalade

1 large duck

Preheat the oven to 350 degrees. Boil the water in a medium saucepan. Add 4 of the tea bags and steep 3 to 5 minutes. Remove the tea bags and add the sugar, Grand Marnier or brandy, and cornstarch. Whisk over high heat until thickened. Lower the heat to a simmer and add the orange marmalade. Clean out the duck cavity and line with foil. Place 6 water-dampened tea bags in your duck, pierce the duck several times with a fork, and place on a broiler pan. Glaze the duck with marmalade mix. Cover with foil and bake 25 minutes per pound, reglazing every 15 minutes or so with the pan drippings. When the duck is fully cooked, uncover and glaze it one last time. Raise the oven temperature to 425 degrees, and continue baking for 10 minutes, or until crispy.

"Strange how a good dinner reconciles everybody."

—Samuel Pepys

PREPARATION TIME
20 MINUTES

COOKING TIME:
25 MINUTES PER
POUND

Cranberry Cove Turkey

SERVES 4

Everyone loves turkey, but who has time to stuff a bird? Luckily, these days you can find turkey tenderloin or breasts as easily as hamburger at the supermarket. This simple, delicious turkey recipe turns any old night into Thanksgiving.

4 cups water

10 Cranberry Cove tea bags

3 pounds turkey tenderloin or
   boneless turkey breasts

2 cups Strawbery Kiwi Cranberry Sauce
   (see page 21) or canned sauce

Place the water, tea bags, and turkey in a large bowl. Cover, refrigerate, and marinate at least 3 hours or, better yet, overnight. Pour 1 cup of the marinade into a shallow baking dish, and discard the remaining marinade. Place the turkey on top. Cover with foil and bake at 350 degrees for 1 hour. Remove the foil and glaze the turkey with 1 cup of the cranberry sauce, reserving the rest for dinner. Put the turkey under the broiler for 5 minutes, or until the sauce is bubbling.

"Thank God for tea! What would the world do without tea? How did it exist? I am glad I was not born before tea."

—Sidney Smith

MARINATE TIME: 3
HOURS OR OVERNIGHT
PREPARATION TIME:
10 MINUTES
COOKING TIME:
1 HOUR

Wild Cherry Blackberry Duck

SERVES 8 TO 10

Most kids' idea of a duck is a toy they play with in the bath. But this dish is so sensational my children cheer when I take it out of the oven. Of course, it will impress your adult friends, too.

3 cups water	1 cup blackberry preserves
1 cup sherry or white wine	1 cup black cherry preserves
13 Wild Cherry Blackberry tea bags	2 ducks, approximately 5 pounds each
2 tablespoons cornstarch	Salt

Preheat the oven to 350 degrees. Boil the water and wine (or sherry) in a saucepan. Add 5 tea bags, lower to a simmer, and steep for 5 minutes. Remove the tea bags, squeezing the excess liquid into the saucepan, and discard. Add the cornstarch to the tea mix, and whisk over high heat until it thickens. Lower to a simmer and add the preserves. Clean out the duck cavities and line them with tin foil. Place 4 dampened tea bags in each. Pierce the ducks several times with a fork. Place on a broiler pan, glaze with some tea mixture, cover with foil, and place in the oven. Roast approximately 25 minutes per pound, reglazing every 15 minutes or so with tea mixture. When fully cooked, uncover the ducks and glaze them well. Raise the temperature to 450 degrees, and roast for another 10 minutes or until crispy.

PREPARATION
TIME:
20 MINUTES
COOKING TIME:
25 MINUTES
PER POUND

Lemon Zinger Chicken Picatta

SERVES 4

My brother T.J. gave me this recipe. He's a wonderful chef, but you'd never know it looking at his apartment. Everything is black: black leather sofa, black chrome lamps, black ceramic table. It's like an ultra-hip funeral home. He served this sophisticated dish to me and a group of his buddies. We all loved it.

3 cups water

4 Lemon Zinger tea bags

4 boneless, skinless chicken breasts,
   pounded (about ½ inch thin)

1 clove garlic, minced

1 cup flour

Salt and pepper

2 tablespoons unsalted butter

4 lemon wedges

Boil the water and carefully pour into a large bowl. Add the tea bags and steep for 10 minutes as the water cools. Remove the tea bags, squeezing excess liquid into bowl, and discard the bags. Add the chicken breasts and garlic, and marinate for at least 20 minutes. Combine the flour and salt and pepper to taste in a large zipper-lock plastic bag. Add the chicken and shake the bag until the chicken is fully coated. Melt the butter in a large frying pan over medium heat. Sauté the chicken on both sides until golden brown and cooked through. Serve garnished with lemon wedges.

"This above all: to thine own self be true, and it must follow, as the night the day, Thou canst not then be false to any man."

—William Shakespeare

MARINATE TIME:
20 MINUTES

PREPARATION TIME:
15 MINUTES

COOKING TIME:
10 TO 15 MINUTES

Almond Sunset Chicken

SERVES 4

This recipe introduced me to the concept of stuffing poultry with tea bags. The flavor of the tea steams the chicken from the inside out as well as the outside in. Try serving the dipping sauce in little tea cups on the side for added drama.

1 large roasting chicken

8 Almond Sunset tea bags

3 cups water

½ cup honey

4 tablespoons unsalted butter

½ cup slivered almonds

PREPARATION
TIME:
20 MINUTES

COOKING TIME:
20 MINUTES PER
POUND

Rinse the chicken well, both inside and out. Line the cavity with foil, and stuff with 4 water-dampened tea bags. Place the chicken in a large, deep roasting pan, and add the water and the remaining tea bags. Cover loosely with foil and bake 20 minutes per pound at 350 degrees. Uncover the chicken 30 minutes before it's done and carefully spoon out 1 cup of the hot drippings. Combine the drippings, honey, butter, and almonds in a saucepan. Bring to a boil for 5 minutes, stirring often. As the chicken continues to roast, glaze every 5 minutes or so with the sauce until golden brown. Reserve a little sauce for dipping. Carve the chicken and serve.

Orange Mango Chicken

SERVES 4

I love the exciting color contrast between the golden brown chicken and the Orange Mango Sauce! This dish is a perfect and economical main course for an elegant dinner party.

1 cup flour

½ teaspoon garlic powder

½ teaspoon good black
    pepper

4 large boneless skinles chicken
    breasts, cut in half

½ stick (4 tablespoons) butter

3 ½ cups water

4 Orange Mango tea bags

2 teaspoons sherry

¾ cup orange marmalade

"The great thing in this world is not so much where we are, but in what direction we are moving."

—Oliver Wendell Holmes

Combine the flour, garlic powder, black pepper, and chicken breasts in a large zipper-lock plastic bag. Seal and shake well until the chicken is thoroughly coated. Melt the butter in a large frying pan over medium heat. Add the chicken breasts and cook until brown on both sides. Set aside. Boil the water, lower the heat to a simmer, and add the tea bags. Let steep for 5 minutes. Remove the bags and discard. Add the sherry and orange marmalade, and blend evenly. Pour the sauce into a shallow baking dish. Add the chicken. Bake uncovered at 350 degrees for 20 minutes, or until the chicken is cooked through.

PREPARATION
TIME:
 25 MINUTES
COOKING TIME:
20 TO 30 MINUTES

Country Peach Country Chicken

SERVES 4

MARINATE TIME:
4 HOURS TO
OVERNIGHT

PREPARATION TIME:
5 MINUTES

COOKING TIME:
15 TO 20 MINUTES

This dish always brings me back to swinging on the porch at my Aunt Gail's house in Georgia. The combination of pecans and peaches evokes Southern hospitality at its best.

4 cups cold water

8 Country Peach tea bags

4 large boneless, skinless chicken
   breasts

2 large eggs whisked

1 cup chopped pecans

½ stick (4 tablespoons) butter

Country Peach Country Chicken Sauce
   (recipe follows), optional

Place the cold water, tea bags, and chicken breasts in a large bowl. Refrigerate overnight or for no fewer than 4 hours. Place pecans in a large plastic bag. Take each chicken breast, one at a time, dip in egg, place in bag, and shake until fully coated. Melt the butter in a large frying pan or skillet. Add the chicken breasts and fry until golden brown and cooked through (about 7 minutes per side).

Country Peach Country Chicken Sauce

SERVES 4

½ cup water

1 Country Peach tea bag

2 large, ripe, firm peaches

¼ cup cream

Salt

PREPARATION
TIME:
5 MINUTES

COOKING TIME:
10 MINUTES

Boil the water in a small saucepan and add the tea bag. Steep for 5 minutes. Squeeze the excess liquid from the tea bag and discard the bag. Peel, pit, and dice the peaches. Add to the tea and simmer for 5 minutes. Stir in the cream and add salt to taste. Serve over Country Peach Country Chicken (see preceding recipe).

When you're throwing a dinner party and you want to involve your kids, cut out place cards in the shape of a teacup. Then give your children crayons or watercolors, and let them individualize each one. This project always gives me some quiet time to finish cooking and helps Kate and Lucas feel more a part of the preparations.

Cranberry Cove Beef Roast

SERVES 4

Nobody makes a meaner pot roast than my grandmother Kay. Well, maybe it's a tie, now that I've added Cranberry Cove tea to jazz up this Yankee tradition.

2 tablespoons vegetable oil

2 ½–3 pound boneless beef rump roast

3 cups water

3 Cranberry Cove tea bags

2 diced shallots plus 1 diced shallot
   for studding the roast

1 (16-ounce) can whole-berry
   cranberry sauce

½ cup sherry

1 tablespoon black pepper

Salt

3 tablespoons cornstarch

PREPARATION TIME:
25 MINUTES

COOKING TIME:
3½ HOURS

Put the oil in a large frying pan. Add the roast and brown on both sides. Transfer the roast to a large roasting pan. Bring the water to a boil in a saucepan. Add the tea bags, steep for 5 minutes, remove and discard. Stud the roast with 1 diced shallot. Pour the cranberry sauce over the top. Pour the tea into the pan. Add the remaining shallots and the sherry and black pepper. Add salt to taste. Roast at 325 degrees for 3 to 3 1/2 hours. Set the roast on a cutting board and slice. Pour the tea drippings into a saucepan, whisk in the cornstarch, and boil until thickened for gravy.

Cinnamon Apple Spice Pork Tenderloin

I threw a fund-raiser for the governor of Colorado, Roy Romer in 1994. When planning the event, I asked what the governor would like for dinner. His assistant replied, "Well, he's pretty tired of those fancy Washington dinners where you get four strands of pasta and a sundried tomato. What he'd really like is some meat and potatoes." So that's what he got. P.S. Not that I'm taking credit, but he was reelected.

½ cup brown sugar

1 tablespoon ground black pepper

1 ½ to 2 pounds pork tenderloin

2 tablespoons butter

1 cup water

2 Cinnamon Apple Spice tea bags

Cinnamon Apple Spice Chutney
   (recipe follows)

Combine the brown sugar and black pepper. Roll the pork tenderloin in the mixture. Melt the butter in a frying pan, add the pork, and turn often over medium heat until browned. Place the tenderloin, water, and tea bags in a baking dish, cover with foil, and roast at 325 degrees for 1 hour. Slice and serve with Cinnamon Apple Spice Chutney.

"Nurture your mind with great thoughts, for you will never go any higher than you think."

—Benjamin Disraeli

PREPARATION TIME:
15 MINUTES

COOKING TIME:
1 HOUR

Cinnamon Apple Spice Chutney

SERVES 4

This tasty chutney keeps for a couple of weeks in the fridge, and it's so versatile. It's great for gussying up plain old pork chops or spooned hot over vanilla ice cream. And it makes the house smell wonderful.

2 cups water

2 Cinnamon Apple Spice
   tea bags

½ cup raisins

6 Macintosh apples, chopped (no need to
   peel or core), or you can use Granny
   Smith for a tarter flavor

½ cup chopped walnuts

Boil the water in a heavy saucepan, add the tea bags, lower to a simmer, and steep for 5 minutes. Remove and discard the tea bags. Add the remaining ingredients. Cook for at least 1 hour, stirring often, until you get the desired texture, thick and chunky.

PREPARATION
TIME:
10 MINUTES
COOKING TIME:
1 HOUR

Firelight Orange Spice Pork Chops

SERVES 4

I served this dish to some friends. We'd been skiing in a snowstorm. Everyone was tired, cold, cranky, and starving. Eyes lit up when this dish came out of the oven. Suddenly, it became one of the best days we'd ever had.

4 thick, American cut pork chops

2 tablespoons vegetable oil

1 cup water

2 Firelight Orange Spice tea bags

¾ cup orange marmalade

¼ cup diced scallions

¼ cup cooking sherry

½ teaspoon sugar

½ teaspoon salt

Brown the pork chops in oil on both sides, and place in a baking dish. Boil the water in a saucepan, add the tea bags, lower to a simmer and steep for 5 minutes. Remove and discard the tea bags. Add the remaining ingredients to the saucepan, and bring to a boil, stirring often for 10 minutes. Pour the sauce over the pork chops, and bake for 1 hour at 300 degrees.

"Friendship is a serious affection; the most sublime of all affections, because it is founded on principle, and cemented by time."

—Mary Wollstonecraft Shelley

PREPARATION TIME:
20 MINUTES

COOKING TIME:
1 HOUR

Wild Cherry Blackberry Pork Tenderloin

SERVES 4

MARINATE TIME:
3 HOURS OR
OVERNIGHT

PREPARATION TIME:
25 MINUTES

COOKING TIME:
1 HOUR

My whole neighborhood taste-tested this one. Even my finicky neighbor John and my friend Wendy's picky 4-year-old gave this dish a thumbs-up.

3 cups water

¼ cup white vinegar

2 pork tenderloins, totaling about 2 pounds

8 Wild Cherry Blackberry tea bags

2 tablespoons vegetable oil

¼ cup diced shallots

¼ cup sherry or red wine

1 cup plum or blackberry jam

1 teaspoon sugar

Combine the water, vinegar, pork, and tea bags in a large bowl. Cover and refrigerate overnight, or at least 3 hours. Brown the tenderloins in the oil in a large baking dish. Set aside. In the same pan, sauté the shallots until clear. Add the vinegar marinade and sugar. Slice a pocket into each tenderloin lengthwise and stuff with the shallots. Pour the sherry into the same pan, bring to a boil, lower the heat to a simmer, and blend in the preserves. Pour the glaze over the pork, cover with foil, and bake at 325 degrees for 1 hour.

Apricot Ginger Ham Glaze

SERVES 4

Apricot and ginger are a welcome change from the more traditional orange glazes used for ham. This glaze is also lovely on any cut of pork.

½ cup water

2 Apricot Ginger tea bags

¾ cup apricot preserves

1 tablespoon fresh ginger, peeled and chopped

1 tablespoon cooking sherry

Bring the water to a boil. Add the tea bags and simmer for 5 minutes. Remove the tea bags and discard. Add the remaining ingredients and stir on a simmer until blended.

"It is one of the most beautiful compensations of life that no man can sincerely try to help another without helping himself."

—Ralph Waldo Emerson

PREPARATION TIME:
20 MINUTES

English Breakfast Beef Stew

SERVES 4

"Cheerfulness keeps up a kind of daylight in the mind, and fills it with a steady and perpetual serenity."

—Joseph Addison

Beef meets its match in the hearty flavor of English Breakfast tea. Just be sure to use a good cut, since you're not marinating and tenderizing the beef beforehand.

6 cups water

6 English Breakfast tea bags

¼ cup vegetable oil

1 ½ pounds beef, cubed (rump roast is good, you can even use London broil)

1 large onion, sliced

2 cups carrots, peeled and cut into large pieces (4 carrots)

2 cups potatoes (skins on), cut into large cubes (approximately ¾ pound)

1 ½ tablespoons salt

1 tablespoon pepper

½ cup grated cheddar, optional

PREPARATION TIME:
30 MINUTES
COOKING TIME:
2 HOURS

Boil the water and steep the tea bags for 10 minutes. Remove the tea bags and discard. Pour the oil into a large, heavy pot. Brown the beef and onions in the oil. Lower the heat to a simmer and add the carrots, potatoes, salt, pepper, and tea. Let simmer for 90 minutes, or until the potatoes are tender. Serve in warm bowls topped with grated cheddar, if desired.

Lemon Zinger Sea Bass with Zinger Salsa

SERVES 4

Why on earth would anyone poach fish in tap water, when they can poach it in Lemon Zinger Tea? Your fish will be perfectly seasoned and deliciously lemony. And the hibiscus in the tea gives the bass a lovely delicate pink hue. The zesty lemon and the cool cucumbers make a sensational contrast in the salsa.

5 Lemon Zinger tea bags

½ cup vinegar

¾ cup diced plum tomatoes

½ cup diced cucumbers

3 tablespoons chopped chives

2 cups water

4 sea bass filets

"It is only in sorrow bad weather masters us; in joy we face the storm and defy it."

—Amelia Barr

PREPARATION TIME: 25 MINUTES

CHILL TIME: 30 MINUTES

COOKING TIME: 15 TO 20 MINUTES

To prepare the salsa, steep 1 of the tea bags in the vinegar in a bowl for 15 to 20 minutes. Remove the tea bag, squeezing out excess vinegar, and discard. Add the tomatoes, cucumbers, and chives. Chill for at least 1/2 hour. To prepare the fish, bring the water to a boil in a large saucepan, add the 4 remaining tea bags, lower to a simmer and steep for 4 minutes. Remove and discard the tea bags. Gently lay the fish filets in the tea. Simmer for 7 to 10 minutes, or until cooked through. Carefully remove the filets and serve topped with the Zinger salsa.

Firelight Orange Spice Beef

SERVES 4

Orange beef is one of my favorite Chinese dishes. American cooking rarely pairs meat with fruit, but the two are sensational together. Marinating an inexpensive cut like London broil in tea adds wonderful sweet, sour, and spicy notes to the beef all at once.

1 ½–2 pound London broil	1 tablespoon soy sauce
4 cups lukewarm water	2 tablespoons brown sugar
4 Firelight Orange Spice tea bags	1 teaspoon black pepper
¼ cup orange marmalade	1 teaspoon salt

Place the London broil, water, and tea bags in a large bowl. Cover, refrigerate, and marinate overnight, or for no fewer than 3 hours. Combine the remaining ingredients in a saucepan over medium heat. Simmer for 10 minutes. Coat the meat with the glaze, and broil or grill, reglazing often, until cooked to your liking. Slice at an angle and serve.

MARINATE TIME:
3 HOURS OR
OVERNIGHT
PREPARATION TIME
10 MINUTES
COOKING TIME:
15 MINUTES

Misty Mango Salsa over Swordfish

SERVES 2

It's as easy to grill a swordfish steak as it is a burger. The brilliant tropical color and flavor of Misty Mango is the perfect complement for the firm white slabs of swordfish. You can make the salsa ahead of time (it's even better after it has steeped awhile).

2 Misty Mango tea bags

½ cup white vinegar

2 mangoes, peeled and cubed

½ red pepper, diced small

4 tablespoons chopped chives

2 swordfish steaks (approximately ½ pound each)

To make the salsa, steep the tea bags in the vinegar for 20 minutes. Remove and discard the bags, squeezing the excess liquid into the tea. Toss the mangoes, red pepper, and chives in a bowl. Add 1/4 cup of the tea vinegar. Set aside. Brush the swordfish steaks with the remaining vinegar and grill to your liking. Top each steak with 2 tablespoons of the mango salsa and serve.

"Always do right—this will gratify some and astonish the rest."

—Mark Twain

PREPARATION TIME: 25 MINUTES

COOKING TIME: 10 TO 15 MINUTES

Grilled Tuna with Strawberry Kiwi Salsa

SERVES 4

Most of us parents assume our kids' appreciation of seafood stops at fish sticks. But when I grilled these tuna steaks and topped them with the Strawberry Kiwi salsa, Lucas and Kate couldn't get enough.

2 Strawberry Kiwi tea bags	1 ½ teaspoons sugar
¼ cup white vinegar	3 peeled, diced kiwis
4 tablespoons light soy sauce	½ cup diced strawberries
1 teaspoon minced garlic	¼ cup fresh chopped cilantro

To prepare the salsa, steep the tea bags in the vinegar for 15 minutes. Remove the bags, squeezing out the excess liquid, and discard the bags. Add the soy sauce, garlic, sugar, kiwis, cilantro, and strawberries and toss. Set aside. Grill the tuna steaks to your liking. Top each steak with a few tablespoons of the salsa, and enjoy.

PREPARATION TIME:
25 MINUTES

COOKING TIME:
15 TO 20 MINUTES

Bengal Spice Shrimp

PREPARATION TIME:
30 MINUTES

MARINATE TIME:
2 TO 3 HOURS

COOKING TIME:
10 MINUTES

This dish is ideal fancy dinner party food: Your guests will feel as if they're dining on the Orient Express. This is one of my most special dishes, but it's a snap to make with tea. Serve it over white rice.

3 cups water

8 Bengal Spice tea bags

1 pound large raw shrimp, peeled
  and deveined

2 tablespoons butter

1 cup diced green peppers (1 large pepper)

¾ cup diced yellow onions (1 medium onion)

½ cup sliced water chestnuts

1 pint heavy cream

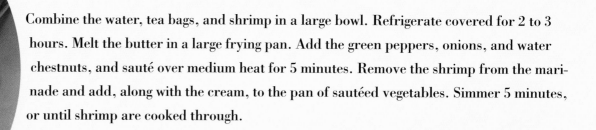

Combine the water, tea bags, and shrimp in a large bowl. Refrigerate covered for 2 to 3 hours. Melt the butter in a large frying pan. Add the green peppers, onions, and water chestnuts, and sauté over medium heat for 5 minutes. Remove the shrimp from the marinade and add, along with the cream, to the pan of sautéed vegetables. Simmer 5 minutes, or until shrimp are cooked through.

Apricot Ginger Shrimp

SERVES 4

This dish is my take on a sweet-and-sour Chinese classic, without the cardboard takeout boxes.

3 tablespoons wok or peanut oil

¼ cup diced scallions, (approximately 4 without bulbs)

3 Apricot Ginger tea bags

1 ½ cups water

2 teaspoons light soy sauce

¼ cup apricot preserves

½ teaspoon salt

2 tablespoons cornstarch

2 pounds shrimp, peeled and deveined

Put the oil in a large wok. Add the scallions and sauté over medium heat for a few minutes. Steep the tea bags in the water in a separate container. Remove and discard the tea bags. Add the tea to the wok, along with the soy sauce, apricot preserves, and salt. Whisk in the cornstarch, cooking until the sauce is slightly thickened. Add the shrimp and simmer until pink and cooked through.

Next time you're enjoying the great outdoors, surprise your hiking partner with an afternoon tea. Some fancy napkins, pretty tea cups, and dainty sandwiches weigh only a little more than a few Power Bars, but think of the impact.

PREPARATION TIME:
20 MINUTES

COOKING TIME:
10 MINUTES

Apricot Ginger Salmon

SERVES 4

My girlfriend Nancy has been poaching salmon filets in juice for years. But she has to buy the whole fruit stand! I simplified her recipe by using Apricot Ginger tea instead.

4 cups water

6 Apricot Ginger tea bags

2 teaspoons minced fresh garlic

5 tablespoons sesame oil

4 salmon filets (1 ½–2 pounds)

2 tablespoons light soy sauce

Bring the water to a boil, add the tea bags, and set aside to steep for 5 minutes. Pour the sesame oil into a large frying pan. Sauté the garlic over medium heat for a few minutes. Add the salmon (pink side down). Cook for 4 minutes; then gently turn the filets over. Remove and discard the tea bags. Add the soy sauce to the tea. Pour over the salmon, cover, and cook another 5 minutes, or until fish is cooked through.

PREPARATION TIME:
10 MINUTES

COOKING TIME:
10 MINUTES

Desserts

So many of our teas are blended not only with exotic herbs and spices, but with delectable fruits as well—what better marriage with any dessert recipe? Some recipes are light, all are luscious.

Vanilla Hazelnut Fruit and Bread Pudding

SERVES 4

This recipe is a tribute to Lorraine Cappello, a lovely woman and superb Lebanese cook. I served this as a special surprise to her daughter, Ramona, and happy memories of her childhood flowed through the room.

1 (12-inch) loaf of French
    bread, toasted and cubed
½ cup raisins
¼ cup chopped walnuts
2 apples, cored, peeled,
    and diced

1 banana, sliced
2 Vanilla Hazelnut tea bags
2 cups water
1 cup brown sugar
¾ cup cream, optional

PREPARATION TIME:
15 MINUTES
COOKING TIME:
30 MINUTES

Combine the toast cubes, raisins, walnuts, apples, and bananas in a large mixing bowl. Bring the water to a boil in a saucepan, add the tea bags and steep for 4 minutes. Remove the tea bags, squeezing out the excess liquid, and discard the bags. Add the brown sugar to the tea and stir until dissolved. Pour the sugared tea into the fruit and toast mix and let set for 5 minutes. Pour into a baking dish and bake at 325 degrees for 30 minutes. Serve with cream, if desired.

Raspberry Zinger Dessert Sauce

SERVES 4

Pound cake just too plain? Chocolate cake with a scoop of vanilla ice cream just isn't special enough? You can give any dessert new zing with this incredible sauce.

2 cups water

2 Raspberry Zinger tea bags

½ cup sugar

⅔ cup heavy cream, whipped

1 cup fresh raspberries

Bring the water and tea bags to a boil in a saucepan. Add the sugar and boil down to a syrupy texture, stirring occasionally. You should have about 1 cup of liquid. This should take 20 to 30 minutes. Remove from the heat and fold in the whipped cream and raspberries. Serve over pound cake, chocolate cake, or ice cream.

Why not try arranging flowers in a teapot instead of a traditional vase?
It makes for a beautiful, elegant, whimsical centerpiece.

"The value of life lies not in the length of days, but in the use we make of them...."

—Montaigne

COOKING TIME:
20 TO 30 MINUTES

Wild Cherry Blackberry Rice Pudding

"People don't notice whether it's winter or summer when they're happy."

—Anton Chekhov

Every New Yorker who's ever spent time in a deli loves rice pudding, and I'm no exception. I couldn't wait to find just the right tea to enhance the pudding, and after many experiments, this is by far my favorite. P.S. It's purple!

3 cups water

4 Wild Cherry Blackberry
   tea bags

1 ½ cups white rice

1 cup sugar

1 cup heavy cream, whipped

Fresh blackberries for garnish

COOKING TIME:
30 MINUTES
CHILLING TIME:
1 HOUR

Bring the water to a boil in a heavy saucepan, add the tea bags and continue to boil for 4 minutes. Remove the tea bags, squeezing out excess, and discard the bags. Add the rice, lower to a simmer, and cover. Cook for 20 minutes, or until rice is tender. Stir in the sugar, then the whipped cream. Re-cover and simmer for another 5 minutes. Pour the pudding into a large bowl and chill for 1 hour. Garnish with fresh berries and serve.

Vanilla Hazelnut Poached Pears

SERVES 4

You can't fail to make a brilliant impression on your guests with this sumptuous, sophisticated dessert. I present it two ways and both are quite dramatic. You can stand the whole pear in a goblet. (It looks great, but it is difficult to eat this way.) Or you can slice the pear thinly and arrange it on a dessert plate swimming in the sauce. What a taste treat!

3 Vanilla Hazelnut tea bags

4 cups water

¾ cup brown sugar

¾ cup white sugar

⅔ cup sherry or white wine

4 ripe yet firm pears

Combine the ingredients in a large saucepan, adding the pears last. Simmer for 10 to 20 minutes until the pears are tender. Remove the pears and place them in wine goblets or dessert bowls. Remove and discard the tea bags, and bring the liquid to a boil. Boil down to 2 cups (this should take about 30 minutes). Pour the sauce evenly over the pears, and serve either warm or cold.

"This action is best which procures the greatest happiness for the greatest numbers."

—Francis Hutcheson

COOKING TIME:
40 TO 50 MINUTES

Harvest Spice Tea Cake

SERVES 6-8

I like serving this cake straight from the oven with a steaming pot of Harvest Spice tea. The warm, deep golden color of the whipped cream makes this the ultimate breakfast or teatime treat.

½ cup water

2 Harvest Spice tea bags

3 eggs

¾ cup sugar

1 teaspoon vanilla

1 ¼ cups flour

1 ½ teaspoons baking powder

½ teaspoon salt

Pinch of nutmeg for garnish

Butter for greasing the pan and for garnish

Harvest Spice Whipped Cream (recipe follows)

PREPARATION TIME:
10 MINUTES
COOKING TIME:
25 MINUTES

Preheat the oven to 350 degrees. Bring the water to a boil in a saucepan, add the tea bags, and steep for 3 to 5 minutes. Mix the remaining ingredients in a large bowl. Add the tea, carefully squeezing excess liquid from tea bags before discarding the bags. Blend the batter well. Pour into an 8 x 8 x 2-inch greased baking dish. Bake for 25 minutes. Serve warm, buttered and sprinkled with nutmeg. Top with dollops of Harvest Spice whipped cream.

Harvest Spice Whipped Cream

1 cup whipping cream

2 Harvest Spice tea bags

2 tablespoons sugar

Nutmeg for garnish

"...the lark may never refuse her song, if the true sun should dawn."

—Margaret Fuller

Simmer the cream and tea bags in a small pot for 6 to 10 minutes. Remove the tea bags, squeezing out the excess cream, and discard the bags. Mix the cream and sugar together in a large bowl. Whip until fluffy. Serve with a sprinkle of nutmeg.

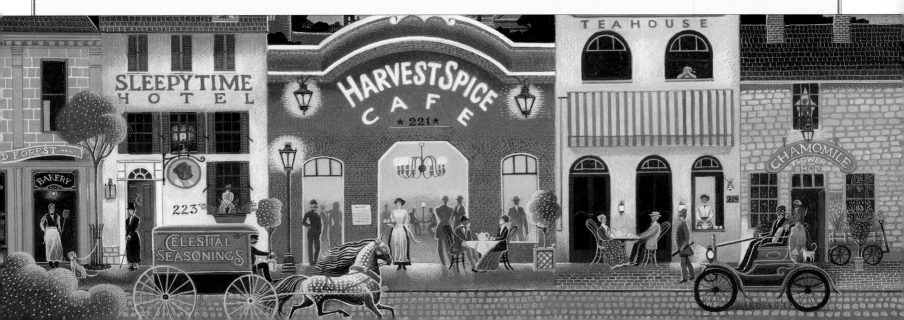

Wild Cherry Blackberry Dessert Sauce

SERVES 4

"While it lies in our
power to do, it lies in
our power not to do."

—Aristotle

Try this low-fat alternative to heavy, creamy dessert sauce over frozen yogurt.

3 cups water
4 Wild Cherry Blackberry
   tea bags

1 cup sugar
1 pound (about 3 cups) blackberries, pitted
   cherries, or both, fresh or frozen

Boil the water and steep the tea bags for 10 minutes. Discard the tea bags. Add the sugar, and continue to boil, stirring often until the mixture is reduced by one-third (about 20 minutes). Add the fruit and simmer for another 10 minutes. Pour over your favorite ice cream, pound cake, or anything else you like.

PREPARATION AND
COOKING TIME:
40 MINUTES

Nutcracker Sweet Pie

SERVES 6-8

I like to make this pie with hazelnuts, pecans and walnuts but any combination is great. For a southwestern version add a handful of pine nuts.

PREPARATION AND
COOKING TIME:
60 TO 75 MINUTES

2 Nutcracker Sweet tea bags

1 cup boiling water

2 ounces unsweetened chocolate

⅓ cup butter

1 ½ cups sugar

½ teaspoon salt

1 cup mixed unsalted nuts,
  chopped

2 eggs

1 pie crust

In a saucepan steep two Nutcracker Sweet tea bags in boiling water for 4 minutes. Remove and discard the tea bags. Lower the heat to a simmer. Add chocolate and butter, stirring until melted. Remove the saucepan from the heat and let it cool for 10 minutes. Add sugar, salt, nuts and eggs and mix well. Pour this mixture into a pie shell. Bake in a preheated oven for 45 minutes. Serve warm or cold, alone or with whipped cream.

Vanilla Maple Pudding

SERVES 6

COOKING TIME:
20 MINUTES
CHILLING TIME:
1 HOUR

When I needed more delicious desserts for the book I went to Patty Bardenett, who runs the Celestial Café. If you're ever in Boulder, you should drop by. What started as a corporate cafeteria has turned into one of the most charming lunch spots in town. When was the last time you broke bread in a tea box? The following are eight of Patty's favorite recipes that you might enjoy on any given day in the café.

5 cups cold milk

8 Vanilla Maple tea bags

¾ cup sugar

⅓ cup cornstarch

Warm 4 cups of the milk in a saucepan over medium heat. Add the tea bags and steep for 5 minutes. Remove the tea bags, squeezing out the excess milk, and discard the bags. Stir in the sugar and remove from the heat. Put the remaining cup of cold milk and the cornstarch in a jar. Shake until smooth. Whisk this mixture into the tea milk and sugar; then return to medium heat. Whisk continuously until thickened. Pour the pudding into dessert bowls or, even better, tea cups, and chill for at least 1 hour.

Strawberry Kiwi Tart

DOUGH:

6 tablespoons butter

1 cup flour

1 egg yolk

2 tablespoons water

Butter for greasing the pan

Cut the butter into the flour in a large bowl. Blend with a pastry blender or knead by hand. Whisk the egg yolk, and blend in the water. Add to the flour and mix. Roll into a ball. Wrap in plastic and refrigerate for 20 minutes. Preheat the oven to 425 degrees. Roll out the dough and press it into a lightly greased tart pan. Bake for 12 to 15 minutes and cool before filling.

FILLING AND GLAZE:

½ cup water

2 Strawberry Kiwi tea bags

½ cup sugar

2 tablespoons cornstarch

2 cups sliced strawberries

2 peeled and sliced kiwis

Bring the water and tea bags to a boil in a heavy saucepan, reduce to a simmer, and steep for 5 minutes. Remove the tea bags, squeeze out the excess, and discard. Add the sugar and cornstarch, and whisk over high heat until thickened. Remove from heat. Arrange the fruit slices in the tart shell. Pour the cooled glaze over tart. Let stand for 20 minutes and serve.

"Great necessities call out great virtues."

—Abigail Adams

CRUST:
PREPARATION TIME:
30 MINUTES
COOKING TIME:
12 TO 15 MINUTES

FILLING/GLAZE:
PREPARATION TIME:
10 MINUTES
COOLING TIME:
20 MINUTES

Cinnamon Apple Crisp

SERVES 8

1 cup water

4 Cinnamon Apple tea bags

6 cups cored, sliced apples

⅓ cup brown sugar

½ cup flour

2 tablespoons butter

TOPPING:

1 cup flour

⅓ cup oatmeal

4 tablespoons brown sugar

4 tablespoons softened butter

COOKING TIME:
1 HOUR

Bring the water to a boil in a heavy saucepan, add the tea bags and steep for 5 minutes. Remove and discard the tea bags. Place the apples in an 11 x 7-inch baking dish. Sprinkle with the brown sugar and flour, dot with the butter, and pour the tea over the top. Combine the topping ingredients in a small mixing bowl, and blend with a pastry mixer or by hand until uniformly smooth. Spread evenly over the top of the apples. Bake covered with foil at 350 degrees for 45 minutes. Then uncover and continue to bake for another 15 minutes.

Wild Cherry Blackberry Cake

SERVES 6-8

1 cup water

6 Wild Cherry Blackberry tea bags

1 stick (8 tablespoons) butter plus
   butter for greasing the pan

1 cup sugar

3 eggs

1 cup mini chocolate chips

2 ⅓ cups flour

1 ½ teaspoons baking powder

½ teaspoon baking soda

Bring the water to a boil in a heavy saucepan, add the tea bags, remove from the heat and steep for 5 minutes. Remove the tea bags, squeezing out excess liquid, and discard the bags. Set the tea aside. Cream the butter and sugar in a large bowl. Mix in the eggs one at a time. Add the tea (which should be room temperature) and blend well. Add the remaining ingredients and mix thoroughly. Pour into a well-greased bundt pan. Bake at 350 degrees for 35 minutes, or until a toothpick comes out clean.

"How pleasant it is, at the end of the day, no follies to have to repent; But reflect on the past, and be able to say, That my time has been properly spent."
—Jane Taylor

PREPARATION TIME:
20 MINUTES
COOKING TIME:
35 MINUTES

Wild Cherry Blackberry Cake Sauce

COOKING TIME:
10 MINUTES

¼ cup water

1 Wild Cherry Blackberry
   tea bag

½ cup chocolate chips

3 tablespoons cherry or
   blackberry preserves

Bring the water to a boil in a heavy saucepan. Add the tea bag. Remove from the heat and steep for 4 minutes. Remove the tea bag, squeezing out the excess liquid, and discard the bag. Return the saucepan to very low heat, and add the chocolate and preserves slowly, stirring constantly until melted. Pour this wonderful sauce over the top of your cake and serve.

Apricot Ginger Bread

SERVES 12

1 cup water

4 Apricot Ginger tea bags

1 cup softened butter

1 cup brown sugar

1 cup honey

3 eggs

2 ½ cups flour

½ teaspoon baking powder

Bring the water to a boil in a heavy saucepan. Add the tea bags and continue to boil for 5 minutes. Remove and discard the bags. Place the butter, sugar, and honey in a large mixing bowl. Pour the tea over, and whisk until the butter is melted and slightly cooled. Beat the eggs, and add. Then stir in the dry ingredients and beat until smooth. Pour into a buttered (or any non-stick sprayed) 9 x 13-inch pan, and bake at 350 degrees for 50 to 60 minutes until done.

This gingerbread stays moist for days!

"Nothing contributes so much to tranquilize the mind as a steady purpose—a point on which the soul may fix its intellectual eye."

—Mary Wollstonecraft Shelley

PREPARATION TIME: 20 MINUTES
COOKING TIME: 50 TO 60 MINUTES

Country Peach Passion Cobbler

SERVES 6-8

*"Joy is not in things.
It is in us."*

—Richard Wagner

PREPARATION TIME:
20 MINUTES

COOKING TIME:
45 MINUTES

3 cups water

8 Country Peach Passion tea bags

4 cups sliced peaches, fresh
   or frozen

¾ cup sugar

4 tablespoons cornstarch

TOPPING:

2 cups Bisquick baking mix

3 tablespoons sugar

1 cup milk

1 egg

Bring the water to a boil in a heavy saucepan. Add the tea bags and continue to boil for 5 minutes. Remove and discard the tea bags. Place the peaches in a 9 x 13-inch baking pan, and sprinkle the sugar and cornstarch over the top. Then add the tea. Blend the topping ingredients in a mixing bowl until a dough is formed. Drop the dough 1 tablespoon at a time evenly over the peaches. Bake at 350 degrees for 45 minutes until golden brown.

Peppermint Chocolate Cake

SERVES 8

1 cup water

6 Peppermint tea bags

3 ounces unsweetened chocolate
    broken into pieces

½ cup soft butter, plus enough
    butter to grease the pan

2 cups sugar

2 eggs, separated

1 ½ teaspoons baking soda

1 ¼ cup sour cream

2 cups flour, plus enough to dust pan

1 teaspoon Baking powder

Powdered sugar for dusting cake

"Goodness is the only
investment that never
fails."

—Henry David Thoreau

PREPARATION TIME:
30 MINUTES
COOKING TIME:
40 MINUTES

Preheat the oven at 350 degrees. Bring the water to a boil in a heavy saucepan, add the tea bags, remove from the heat and steep for 5 minutes. Remove the tea bags, squeezing out the excess, and discard the bags. Return the tea to a boil. Combine the chocolate and butter in a large bowl. Pour the tea over the top. Whisk until melted. Stir in the sugar and egg yolks. In a separate bowl, mix the baking soda and sour cream. Add to the batter and mix well. Next, sift the flour and baking powder into the batter and mix well. Whip the egg whites until stiff in a separate bowl. Fold into the batter. Grease and flour one bundt pan. Pour in the batter. Bake for 40 minutes. Sprinkle with powdered sugar.

Iced & Hot Teas

I'm a bit of a Puritan and a purist at heart: I think the best way to enjoy Celestial Seasonings teas is straight up. But Mo has always liked to experiment with his beverages. At home we call him the Professor of Mixology. With these recipes, you too can earn your doctorate.

Zingerade

This beverage is served every day at the Celestial Cafe in Boulder, Colorado, and it's a real favorite.

4 Red Zinger tea bags

1 quart warm water

1 quart cold water

12 ounces frozen lemonade

½ cup sugar

Place the tea bags in a half-gallon pitcher and add the warm water. Place the pitcher in the refrigerator and steep for 1 hour. Remove the tea bags, add the remaining ingredients, and stir well.

Earl Grey Orange Cooler

SERVES 1

This is a sophisticated, adult beverage without alcohol. I like to serve this drink at alfresco dinner parties with fancy grilled foods. The bergamot in the Earl Grey is flavorful enough to stand up to any barbecue.

1 cup water

1 Earl Grey tea bag

½ cup orange juice

Ice Cubes

Boil the water and remove from the heat. Add the tea bag, steep for 3 minutes, remove, and discard. Cool the tea and pour into a tall glass. Add the orange juice and ice to fill. Stir until chilled.

Strawberry Kiwi Soda

SERVES 8

You won't believe what a few tea bags will do for plain old soda. It looks gorgeous in a punch bowl with strawberries and kiwi slices floating on top.

1 (2-liter) bottle Sprite or 7-Up   **5 Strawberry Kiwi tea bags**

Pour out 1 cup of soda from a full bottle and drink or save. Slowly add the tea bags one at a time to the bottle. Replace the cap on bottle and refrigerate for at least 30 minutes.

Strawberry Kiwi Slushy

SERVES 2

Dazzle your kids with this all-natural, healthful version of their favorite slushy.

Crushed ice   **$\frac{1}{2}$ cup strawberries, stems**
2 Strawberry Kiwi tea bags   **removed (approximately $\frac{1}{4}$ pound)**
2 cups water   **1 kiwi, peeled and sliced**
                                         $\frac{1}{2}$ cup sugar

Boil water, remove from heat and steep tea bags for five minutes. Place the ice in the blender until it is about three-quarters full. Add the remaining ingredients and puree until smooth.

Orange Mango Zinger Party Punch

SERVES 12

This sassy punch provides a wake-up call to the palate. Float fruit slices on top to jazz it up.

6 cups water	3 cups mango juice
6 Orange Mango tea bags	3 cups ginger ale

Bring the water to a boil. Carefully pour into a large punch bowl. Steep the tea bags in the water for 5 to 10 minutes, then remove and discard the bags. Add the remaining ingredients, stir, and chill.

Red Zinger Ginger Punch

SERVES 8

5 Red Zinger tea bags	1 (2-liter) bottle ginger ale

Pour out 1 cup of soda, and drink or save. Slowly add the tea bags one at a time to the bottle. Replace the cap and refrigerate for at least 1 hour.

Cinnamon Apple Spice Hot Cider

SERVES 4

After a hard day's work building the perfect snowman, this is a tasty alternative to hot chocolate for your kids.

3 cups water

3 Cinnamon Apple Spice tea bags

2 cups apple juice

4 tablespoons honey

Place the water and tea bags in a saucepan, and bring to a boil. Reduce the heat and simmer, steeping the tea bags for 4 minutes. Remove the bags and discard. Add the juice and honey, and continue to simmer for another 5 minutes. Serve warm.

Harvest Spiced Cider

SERVES 4

When you want a spicy adult twist on the traditional cinnamon-based cider, this version has a real kick.

3 Harvest Spice tea bags

4 cups apple cider

1 cup water

Combine the ingredients in saucepan over medium heat, and simmer for 10 minutes. Remove the tea bags and serve.

Vanilla Hazelnut La Tea

SERVES 1

As tea's answer to latte, this popular item at the Celestial Café in Boulder is frothy, caffeine-free, and loaded with flavor.

1 ½ cups water

1 Vanilla Hazelnut tea bag

1 teaspoon sugar or ½ packet artificial sweetener

½ cup milk

Bring the water to a boil. Pour carefully into a tall (12-ounce) mug. Steep the tea bag for at least 5 minutes. Discard the bag. Add the sugar or sweetener, and stir. Meanwhile, steam the milk in a cappucino machine. Top off the tea with the steamed milk.

Mandarin Orange Spice Warm Up

SERVES 4

Surprise your friends with this take on an old favorite; they may never go back to hot apple cider.

3 cups water

3 Mandarin Orange Spice tea bags

2 cups orange juice

4 tablespoons honey or sugar

Boil the water in a saucepan. Add the tea bags and simmer for 4 minutes. Remove the bags, and discard. Add the juice and honey or sugar. Continue to simmer for another 5 minutes. Serve immediately.

Happy Teas

*One evening Mo came home after work and pronounced that his taste buds were
in rare form and tonight was "Happy Tea Night." He proceeded to pull out every bottle of
liquor we had in the house, along with twenty or so of our most popular teas. We mixed,
matched, and sipped for hours. Boy, that was a fun night!*

Vanilla Hazelnut Happy Tea

I'll never forget the first time we served this tea. It was at a fancy fund-raiser, and the house was packed with people. Even my parents were there. One of the guests was a beautiful, elegant Catherine Deneuve-type in her late 50s. Well, after several cups of our happy tea, she sashayed up to my father and asked in a smoky voice, "Would you like to see my tattoo?" My father replied, "Yes!" And my mother answered with a resounding "NO!"

3 cups water	**¼ cup Irish cream liqueur**
3 Vanilla Hazelnut tea bags	**¼ cup Frangelico (hazelnut) liqueur**

Bring the water to a boil, and pour into a teapot. Add the tea bags and steep for 5 minutes. Remove the bags, squeezing the excess liquid into the pot, and discard the bags. Add the liqueurs, stir thoroughly, and serve.

Flea markets are my passion and weakness. I never know what new treasure I'm going to unearth. Instead of pricey Irish lace tea napkins, I use some beautiful embroidered handkerchiefs I found while rummaging through a flea market basket! Perfect, elegant, and $1.50 each!

Raspberry Zinger After Dinner Tea

SERVES 1

1 cup water

1 Raspberry Zinger tea bag

1 shot raspberry liqueur (Chambord)

Bring the water to a boil, and pour into a mug. Steep the tea bag for 4 minutes; then discard the bag. Add the liqueur, mix the ingredients, and serve immediately.

Raspberry Zinger Cocktail

SERVES 1

This is a classy cocktail that will bring a blush to your glass and a blush to your cheek.

1 cup water

1 Raspberry Zinger tea bag

¾ shot vodka

1 ½ tablespoons raspberry liqueur (Chambord)

Bring the water to a boil, and pour into a mug. Steep the tea bag for 4 minutes; then discard the bag. Add the vodka and liqueur to the tea. Pour into a tall, ice-filled glass.

Sleepytime Hot Toddy

SERVES 1

Is there anything more relaxing than Sleepytime tea? Maybe this . . .

1 cup water	1 shot scotch or bourbon
1 Sleepytime tea bag	

Boil the water, pour into a mug, and steep the tea for 5 minutes. Remove and discard the tea bag. Add the scotch or bourbon and serve immediately.

Tension Tamer Tension Tamer

SERVES 1

Two parking tickets in one day. Kids home with the chicken pox. Bad day at the office. This soothing brew relaxes you so instantly it's like having a massage in a mug.

1 cup water	1 shot scotch or bourbon
1 Tension Tamer tea bag	

Bring the water to a boil, and pour into a mug. Steep the tea bag for 4 minutes; then discard the bag. Add the scotch or bourbon. Stir and serve immediately.

Nutcracker Sweet

SERVES 1

This Christmas-time tea has scored by far the highest ratings of any tea in our history. Frankly, it doesn't need the liqueurs, but oh, what visions of sugar plum fairies will dance in your head!

1 cup water

1 Nutcracker Sweet tea bag

1 ½ shots Irish cream liqueur

½ shot Amaretto or hazelnut liqueur (Frangelico)

Bring the water to a boil, and pour into a mug. Steep the tea bag for 4 minutes; then discard the bag. Add the liqueurs, stir, and serve immediately.

"Polly, put the kettle on, We'll all have tea."

—Anonymous nursery rhyme

Chamomile Hot Toddy Throat Soother

SERVES 1

Feeling under the weather? This tea will brighten up your night as you snuggle under your quilt.

1 cup water

1 Chamomile tea bag

1 shot bourbon or scotch

2 teaspoons honey

1 lemon wedge

Boil the water, and steep the tea bag for 4 minutes. Remove and discard the bag. Add the bourbon or scotch and honey. Squeeze in the lemon, stir, and serve immediately.

Vanilla Maple Happy Tea

SERVES 1

This tea is like a sundae without the ice cream.

1 cup water

1 Vanilla Maple tea bag

1 ½ shots Irish cream liqueur

½ shot Godiva chocolate liqueur

Bring the water to a boil, and pour into a mug. Steep the tea bag for 4 minutes; then discard the bag. Add the liqueurs, stir, and serve immediately.

Earl Grey Happy Tea

SERVES 1

Earl Grey is a virile tea, bursting with flavor, and the Grand Marnier tames it just enough.

1 cup water

1 Earl Grey tea bag

1 shot Grand Marnier liqueur

Bring the water to a boil, and pour into a mug. Steep the tea bag for 4 minutes; then discard the bag. Add the Grand Marnier, stir, and serve immediately.

"The years teach much which the days never know."

—Ralph Waldo Emerson

Wild Cherry Blackberry Happy Tea

SERVES 1

I admit I never would have thought of combining wild cherries, blackberries, and almonds. Leave it to Mo and his taste buds to invent something as tasty as this.

1 cup water

1 shot Amaretto

1 Wild Cherry Blackberry tea bag

Bring the water to a boil, and pour into a mug. Steep the tea bag for 4 minutes; then discard the bag. Add the Amaretto, stir, and serve immediately.

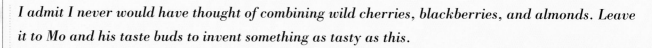

Strawberry Kiwi Margarita Mix

SERVES 15

5 Strawberry Kiwi tea bags

triple sec

1 large jug (59.2) ounces margarita mix

tequila

Pour out 1/2 cup of the margarita mix and discard. Add the 5 Strawberry Kiwi tea bags to the bottle and refrigerate for 2 hours or over night. Shake gently. Remove the tea bags and serve blended with ice, Triple sec and Tequila to taste.

Celestial Seasonings Herb Teas Used in This Book

ALMOND SUNSET
Ingredients: Roasted carob, roasted barley malt, roasted chicory root, cinnamon, natural flavors, anise seed, roasted barley, and orange peel.

BENGAL SPICE
Ingredients: Cinnamon, roasted carob, ginger root, roasted chicory root, dates, cardamon, black pepper, nutmeg, cloves, and quinoa.

CHAMOMILE
Ingredients: Fine chamomile flowers.

CINNAMON APPLE
Ingredients: Cinnamon, hibiscus flowers, roasted chicory root, roasted carob, orange peel, chamomile flowers, natural apple flavor, natural cinnamon flavor, and other natural flavors.

COUNTRY PEACH PASSION
Ingredients: Rosehips, hibiscus flowers, orange peel, roasted chicory root, chamomile flowers, blackberry leaves, natural peach flavor with other natural flavors, natural passionfruit flavor, peaches, and citric acid.

CRANBERRY COVE
Ingredients: Hibiscus flowers, chamomile flowers, cinnamon, roasted chicory root, rosehips, cranberries and apples, dates, licorice root, citric acid and natural flavors.

HARVEST SPICE
Ingredients: Cinnamon, rootbos, roasted chicory root, anise seed, natural flavors, blackberry leaves, hibiscus flowers, orange peel, ginger root, licorice root, and cardamon.

LEMON ZINGER
Ingredients: Hibiscus flowers, rosehips, roasted chicory root, orange peel, lemon grass, lemon peel and whole dried lemons, natural lemon flavor, and citric acid.

MANDARIN ORANGE SPICE
Ingredients: Orange peel, hibiscus flowers, roasted chicory root, rosehips, blackberry leaves, chamomile flowers, hawthorn berries, cinnamon, natural mandarin orange flavor, and other natural flavors, cloves, and coriander.

MINT MAGIC
Ingredients: Spearmint leaves, peppermint leaves, roasted chicory root, cinnamon, and orange peel.

ORANGE MANGO ZINGER
Ingredients: Rosehips, hibiscus flowers, roasted chicory root, orange peel, hawthorn berries, natural orange and mango flavors with other natural flavors, cinnamon, and citric acid.

PEPPERMINT
Ingredients: Peppermint leaves.

RASPBERRY ZINGER
Ingredients: Hibiscus flowers, rosehips, roasted chicory root, blackberry leaves, orange peel, natural raspberry flavor with other natural flavors, lemon grass, raspberries, raspberry leaves, and citric acid.

RED ZINGER
Ingredients: Hibiscus flowers, rosehips, lemon grass, licorice root, natural flavors, and citric acid.

SLEEPYTIME
Ingredients: Chamomile flowers, spearmint leaves, lemon grass, tilia flowers, passionflower leaves, blackberry leaves, orange blossoms, hawthorn berries, and rosebuds.

STRAWBERRY KIWI
Ingredients: Hibiscus flowers, rosehips, orange peel, roasted chicory root, blackberry leaves, natural strawberry and kiwi flavors and other natural flavors, and licorice root.

TENSION TAMER
Ingredients: Eleuthero ginseng root, peppermint leaves, cinnamon, ginger root, chamomile flowers, lemon grass, licorice root, catnip, tilia flowers, natural lemon flavor, hops, and Vitamin B.

WILD CHERRY BLACKBERRY
Ingredients: Hibiscus, rosehips, roasted chicory root, hawthorn berries, blackberry leaves, natural cherry and blackberry flavors with other natural flavors, cinnamon, orange peel, licorice root, and citric acid.

If you need help finding a particular tea or would like our catalog, call 1-800-2000-TEA.

Celestial Seasonings Black Teas Used in This Book

CEYLON APRICOT GINGER

Ingredients: Ceylon and other fine imported black teas, rosehips, ginger root, and natural apricot flavors with other natural flavors.

EARL GREY

Ingredients: Fine imported black tea, natural bergamot flavor, natural rose and orange flavors with other natural flavors, and natural lime flavor.

EMERALD GARDENS

Ingredients: Chinese green tea, Ceylon tea, orange blossoms, ginger root, and natural plum and passionfruit flavors with other natural flavors.

ENGLISH BREAKFAST

Ingredients: Fine imported black tea from Java, Assam, and Kenya.

FIRELIGHT ORANGE SPICE

Ingredients: Fine imported black tea, rosehips, hibiscus flowers, orange peel, natural orange flavors with other natural flavors, cloves, and oranges.

MISTY MANGO

Ingredients: Finest blend of Oolong, Assam, Java, and Kenyan teas, blackberry leaves, natural mango flavor with other natural flavors, hibiscus flowers, marigold petals, and caffeine.

NUTCRACKER SWEET

Ingredients: Fine imported black tea, natural flavors, and cinnamon.

VANILLA MAPLE

Ingredients: Fine imported black tea, roasted barley malt, roasted chicory root, natural vanilla maple flavor and other natural flavors, roasted carob, maple crystals, and vanilla bean.

VANILLA HAZELNUT

Ingredients: Roasted carob, roasted chicory root, cinnamon, roasted barley malt, roasted barley, natural vanilla hazelnut flavor, natural flavors, vanilla bean, and salt.